PhotoPlus X5 User Guide

How to Contact Us

Our main office
(UK, Europe):

The Software Centre
PO Box 2000, Nottingham,
NG11 7GW, UK

Main:	(0115) 914 2000
Registration (UK only):	(0800) 376 1989
Sales (UK only):	(0800) 376 7070
Customer Service/ Technical Support:	http://www.support.serif.com/
General Fax:	(0115) 914 2020

North American office
(USA, Canada):

Serif Inc.,
The Software Center,
4041 MacArthur Blvd., Suite 120,
Newport Beach, CA 92660,
USA

Registration:	(800) 794-6876
Sales:	(800) 489-6703
Customer Service:	(800) 489-6720
Technical Support:	http://www.support.serif.com/

Online

Visit us on the web at: http://www.serif.com/

International

Please contact your local distributor/dealer. For further details, please contact us at one of our phone numbers above.

Credits

This User Guide, and the software described in it, is furnished under an end user License Agreement, which is included with the product. The agreement specifies the permitted and prohibited uses.

Trademarks

Serif is a registered trademark of Serif (Europe) Ltd.

PhotoPlus is a registered trademark of Serif (Europe) Ltd.

All Serif product names are trademarks of Serif (Europe) Ltd.

Microsoft, Windows and the Windows logo are registered trademarks of Microsoft Corporation. All other trademarks acknowledged.

Windows Vista and the Windows Vista Start button are trademarks or registered trademarks of Microsoft Corporation in the United States and/or other countries.

Adobe Photoshop is a registered trademark of Adobe Systems Incorporated in the United States and/or other countries.

Copyrights

Digital Images © 2008 Hemera Technologies Inc. All Rights Reserved.

Digital Images © 2008 Jupiterimages Corporation, All Rights Reserved.

Digital Images © 2008 Jupiterimages France SAS, All Rights Reserved.

Portions Images ©1997-2002 Nova Development Corporation; ©1995 Expressions Computer Software; ©1996-98 CreatiCom, Inc.; ©1996-99 Cliptoart; ©1996-99 Hemera; ©1997 Multimedia Agency Corporation; ©1997-98 Seattle Support Group. Rights of all parties reserved.

Portions graphics import/export technology LEADTOOLS © LEAD Technologies, Inc. All Rights Reserved.

Caroline (cazcarrot) Wilson © 2011, All Rights Reserved.

The Radiance Software License, Version 1.0
Copyright (c) 1990 - 2002 The Regents of the University of California, through Lawrence Berkeley National Laboratory. All rights reserved.

This product includes Radiance software (http://radsite.lbl.gov/) developed by the Lawrence Berkeley National Laboratory (http://www.lbl.gov/).

Table of Contents

1 Welcome

Welcome to PhotoPlus X5

Welcome to **PhotoPlus** X5 from **Serif**—more than ever, the best value in image creation and editing software for any home, school, organization, or growing business. PhotoPlus is the number one choice for working with photographs and paint-type images, whether for the web, multimedia, or the printed page.

PhotoPlus has the features you'll need... from importing or creating pictures, through manipulating colours, making image adjustments, applying filter effects and so much more, all the way to final export. Built-in support for the most modern digital cameras makes it easy to open your very own digital photos, either as JPG or as unprocessed raw images.

PhotoPlus also offers on-computer post-shoot development, using **Raw Studio**, where you're in full control of your raw image's white balance and exposure, and perform "blown" highlight recovery. Raw Studio complements other studios, such as **PhotoFix**, **Filter Gallery**, and **Image Cutout Studio** for image adjustments, filter effects (including stunning artistic effects), and layer cutouts, respectively.

For an overview of PhotoPlus, see Existing features and New features (specific to PhotoPlus X5) on p. 5 and p. 4, respectively.

PhotoPlus and PhotoPlus Organizer: a powerful combination

PhotoPlus takes care of all your image creation and photo editing needs. However, if you're looking to take a step back from photo editing and manage your collection of photos, scanned images, etc. you can use PhotoPlus Organizer (see p. 219). This is installed automatically with PhotoPlus, and offers a powerful platform for launching your photos in PhotoPlus. You'll be able to sort, group, rate, and tag your photos, as well as filter your photos for display by several methods.

Registration

Don't forget to register your new copy, using the **Registration Wizard** on the **Help** menu. That way, we can keep you informed of new developments and future upgrades!

New features

- **Layer Clipping** (see p. 60)
  For more design freedom, clip the contents of an upper layer to a lower layer's contents; simply unclip at any time.

- **Alpha Channel Editing** (see p. 129)
  Create multiple alpha channels for your image—great for channel masking! Selections can also be **stored** as **alpha channels** in the always-at-hand Channels tab, which can be retrieved just when you need them!

- **Improved Adjustments Tab** (see p. 56)
  Reset any adjustment settings back to default. Swap out one adjustment for another—preset or custom—from the adjustment's settings pane.

- **New and Exciting Blend Modes** (see p. 39)
  Additional blend modes include **Lighter Colour**, **Darker Colour**, and **Add**. A new "pass-through" blend mode called **Crossfade** is ideal for keeping adjustment layers in layer groups active in your layer stack.

- **New HSB Colour Mode** (see p. 134)
  Express colours in terms of Hue, Saturation, and Brightness in the Colour tab.

Photo Adjustments (see p. 56)

- **Clarity**
  At project start, add extra sharpness to your photo using the local-contrast **Clarity** adjustment. Slight blurriness is removed in an instant!

- **Vibrance**
  This non-linear adjustment intelligently boosts low-saturation colours while protecting skin tones.

- **Brightness and Contrast**
  Reduced shadow and highlight clipping, along with improvements to midtone contrast, make these adjustments even more essential.

- **HSL**
  Use a **Colour Picker** to sample targeted image areas (e.g., grass, sky, clothing) for more precision during HSL adjustment.

- **Levels and Curves**
  Use **Auto Levels** and **Auto Contrast** on both Levels and Curves adjustments. For curves, sample midtones (e.g., for fine contrast control) directly on your image using an **Add Point** tool, then adjust your curve.

- **Colourize**
  The Colourize adjustment becomes a separate adjustment, offering recolouring of your image.

Existing features

PhotoPlus power

- **Professional Input and Output Options**
  Import an impressive selection of graphic files, including raw images from all the major manufacturers' cameras (and many more...). Support for Photoshop® (.psd), HD Photo, and Corel Paint Shop Pro® import! Export to an equally extensive choice of graphic file formats!

- **Preset Canvas Sizes**
  If you're creating a new picture, adopt a preset **canvas size** selected from Photo, Video, Web, Animation or International/US Paper categories. Alternatively, create your own categories and canvas sizes which can be saved for future use!

- **Versatile Layer Management**
  Create **standard** layers of varying opacity over your **Background** layer. Select, link, merge, arrange, hide, duplicate one or multiple layers all at the same time. Grouping of layers offers easier "bulk" manipulation and better organization. Blend Modes can be applied between layers. Shape and Text layers can be edited at any time; Adjustment and Filter layers offer non-destructive image correction and effects. **Masking** is supported on all layer types.

- **Post-shoot Raw "Development" with Raw Studio**
  Open raw files in Raw Studio and fine tune your work with **white balance**, **exposure**, **noise reduction**, and **chromatic aberration** adjustments. Recover "blown" image highlights with the fantastic **Highlight recovery** feature. A supporting multi-colour histogram aids exposure and recovery control.

- **Unique Selection Options**
  PhotoPlus goes well beyond the basic rectangle, ellipse, freehand, and polygon lasso tools, adding more than a dozen completely customizable selection shapes like polygons, spirals, and stars. Use Magnetic Selection to find edges as you trace them. Or define a selection shaped like text! Create selection areas defined by your laid-down brush strokes; Paint to Select mode lets you literally "brush on" selected areas. Store and load selections between any open file. Use combination buttons (as for shapes) to define cutout selection regions. Adjust any selection using **Feather**, **Smooth**, **Contract**, and **Expand** in combination, all from one location.

- **Crop to Common Print Sizes**
  Use the Crop Tool for easy cropping to different portrait and landscape preset and custom print sizes—print resolution will auto-adjust to honour any print size.

- **Special Erase Options**
  Need to remove that blue sky and leave the clouds? Use the Flood Eraser to fill the blue regions with transparency. Want to isolate a shape from a flat colour background? The Background Eraser samples pixels under the brush, so only unwanted colours drop out.

Colour

- **16-bit Colour Depth/Detail**
  Work in high levels of detail (16-bits/channel) for both RGB and greyscale modes. Each mode can be adopted from scratch or after raw/HD photo import and when outputting HDR merge results.

- **Channels**
  Use PhotoPlus's Channels tab to edit the Red, Green and Blue channels independently.

- **Histogram Support**
  The Histogram tab dynamically responds to show the values for the currently active selection within your document. See how curves and level adjustments affect your image as they happen!

- **Custom and preset colour selection**
  The Colour tab operates in RGB, CMYK, HSL, and Greyscale models for selecting foreground and background colours when painting, creating lines or filling shapes. Use the Swatches tab for themed galleries of preset colour swatches. Use a Web-browser safe category when outputting to the web.

- **Gradient Fills**
  Take your pick of radial, linear, conical, or square fills—perfect for masking, to hide or reveal parts of your photo using smooth graduated blends to transparency. One **master dialog** allows editing of five gradient fill types combining both colour and transparency. Choose from a built-in gallery of presets, add your own categories and fills. (Of course, there's standard flood fill as well.)

- **Professional Colour Management**
  ICC colour profiling means you'll achieve more accurate colours with specific monitors and printers—for printed output that more closely matches on-screen colours.

Brushes, lines and shapes

- **Brushes**
  The **Paintbrush Tool** lets you apply brush strokes using preset brush tips.. choose a tip from basic, calligraphic, and various media categories (watercolour, charcoal, paint, etc.). Stamp and Spray Picture Brush effects and stamps. PhotoPlus lets you create your own category and brush tips! Apply different colours, levels of transparency, blend modes, to any brush, all at varying flow rates. Built-in support for most pressure-sensitive graphics tablets.

- **Freehand and Bézier Curve and Shape Drawing**
  Powerful vector-drawing tools let you produce any shape under the sun with controllable, connectable, editable line segments.

- **Editable QuickShapes**
  Easy to create, easy to change! Simply drag sliders to morph chevrons, hearts, badges, teardrops, moons, zigzags, and many more... apply layer effects and gradient fills... and edit any shape at any time. Create multiple shapes on a single layer—add, subtract, intersect, or exclude with previous shapes for frames, cutouts and custom contours. Draw directly as a Shape layer, path or as a filled bitmap on a raster layer.

- **Paths**
  Use the full range of line- and shape-drawing tools to create editable outlines via the **Paths tab**. Convert paths to or from selections on any layer. "Stroke" paths using any brush to create bordered shapes!

Text

- **Editable Text**
  Add formatted colour text directly onto your image, reposition and scale it by dragging. Text layers keep the contents separate so you can go back and edit selected areas of text or adjust formatting (colour, transparency, etc.) at any time!

Effects

- **Filter Gallery**
  The distort, blur, edge, sharpen, render, stylistic, and artistic effects can be applied singularly or in combination within **Filter Gallery**... guaranteed to keep you up late!

- **Filter Layers**
  Convert to Filter Layer creates a non-destructive layer for powerful control of applied filter effects—switch filter effects on/ off, modify or add to an existing set of filter effects at a later date. Apply to standard or Background layers. For either, your layer content now remains unaffected!
  Automatically create **filter groups** with optional **filter masking**. Apply blend modes and opacity filter-by-filter.

- **Third-party Plug-in Effects and Custom Effects**
  PhotoPlus supports third-party Photoshop® plug-ins, and even lets you design your own custom filters.

- **Layer Effects**
  Add 2D Layer Effects such as **Shadow**, **Glow**, **Bevel**, **Outline** and **Emboss** for a sophisticated look on text or other image elements. Apply multiple effects onto a layer's existing effects for stunning design output. Move into the realm of astounding 3D Lighting and Surface Effects—advanced algorithms bring flat shapes to life! Vary surface and multiple-light source properties. Start with a pattern or a function, adjust parameters for incredible **surface contours, textures, fills**. Use Reflection Maps of indoor/outdoor bitmap environments or **Transparency** control to create realistic glass-like reflective surfaces. Try 3D Painting using Depth Maps to add **instant dimensionality** to your artwork. Painting or erasing on a layer's depth map appears as raised or lowered strokes on the image! Use with 3D layer effects to achieve "carved" side-view textures.

- **Versatile Deform and Warp Tools**
  The "Swiss Army Knife" of image tools, the **Deform Tool** lets you rotate, resize, skew, reshape, or add perspective to any selection or layer. Warp tools pull, stretch, and distort image details, or shrink and enlarge. Pixels turn to putty with the **Mesh Warp Tool**!

- **Merge Bracketed Photos**
  Use **HDR (High Dynamic Range) Merge** to bring together same-shot photos, each taken at different exposure settings. The composite photo, of wider dynamic range, would otherwise be impossible to capture in one shot. Optionally save intermediate HDR images for future use.

Adjustments

- **Image Adjustments**
  Apply professional, darkroom-style colour and histogram adjustments to your images—giving you fingertip control over tones and colours. Adjust Shadow/Highlight/Midtone to calm down overexposed skies in one single operation without having to resort to manipulating curves and levels. Employ the **Blur** and **Sharpen** tools to enhance or reduce local detail... blend multiple layers more cleanly. There's even a dedicated tool for removing "red eye" from flash photos.

- **Editable Adjustment Layers from Adjustments Tab**
  Not only apply colour corrections and special effects, but store each change
  on a separate layer or group. To fine-tune any adjustment later, just click its
  layer and change the settings! Simply select one of an impressive range of
  adjustment presets and you're done! Each preset is designed to correct
  common tonal or colour image deficiencies, every one **customizable** to
  your specific needs.

- **PhotoFix**
  Use for cumulative image adjustments! Adjustments include **White
  Balance**, **Lighting**, and **HSL (Hue/Saturation/Lightness)**. **Straighten** and
  Crop your images—even control **Exposure**. Equally, apply a **Black and
  White Film** effect, **Sharpen**, and fix **Red Eye** and various lens-related
  problems amongst many others. A full-screen dual-image preview display
  lets you compare and fix your images in an instant. Preserve your original
  image layer by creating filter layers directly after **PhotoFix** adjustments. For
  different adjustments on areas of your image, create one or more **masks**—
  each mask storing its own set of editable adjustments!

- **Retouching**
  Clone, Smudge, and Erase tools are included as essential retouch tools. Use
  the PhotoFix's **Blemish Remover** to subtly remove skin blemishes and
  unwanted light reflections—all via blending. For more heavy-duty retouch
  work, use the **Patch Tool** which is especially good for blending out
  irregularly-shaped regions!

- **Quick-and-easy Cutouts**
  Image Cutout Studio makes light work of cutting out parts of your active
  layer. Use brushes to **discard** uniform backgrounds (sky, walls, backdrops)
  or **keep** subjects of interest (people or objects).

Productivity/Workflow

- **Always-at-Hand Tools**
  A **Context toolbar** improves your efficiency by allowing the viewing and editing of a tool's properties in context with the tool currently selected; save and retrieve your favourite tool settings via a Tool Presets tab.

- **Macros**
  Macros let you automate your actions by using a huge number of categorized macro presets—alternatively, record and apply your own macro to any number of photos—give all your photos the same frame, age them or make a colour enhancement all at the same time!

- **Batch Processing**
  Use batch processing to repeat your tasks, e.g. changing file types, all at the same time without user intervention. When used in conjunction with macros the possibilities are endless.

- **Customized Keyboard Shortcuts, Menus and Toolbars**
  Take advantage of customizable keyboard shortcuts—assign your own keystrokes to toolbar and menu commands! Tailor PhotoPlus to your needs with menu, toolbar, and icon customization.

- **Change your Studio Tab Layouts**
  With different **workspaces**, PhotoPlus offers a choice of Studio tab layouts, each designed for specific tasks or users. Alternatively, create your own workspaces!

Web and Animation

- **Image Slicing and Image Maps**
  Now it's not just the pros who can use these techniques to add links to web graphics! Simply click to divide images into segments—each with its own hyperlink and popup text—or add hotspots to specific regions. PhotoPlus outputs the HTML code and lets you preview the results directly in your web browser.

- **Animation Tools**
  It's easy and fun to create or edit animations for the web. You can import and export animated GIFs, apply special effects (including 2D and 3D), tweening, even let PhotoPlus create entire animations for you automatically. Or export to the AVI format for movies and multimedia! **Convert to Animation** makes the process of taking any image into animation mode a breeze!

- **Pixel grid for Web Developers**
  Draw objects and position selection areas with absolute pixel accuracy; benefit from automatic grid display and pixel-by-pixel snapping.

Print and Share

- **Easy Printing**
  Print your project with powerful scaling and tiling options.

- **Print Studio**
  PhotoPlus's unified **Print Studio** allows you to print single images, artistic and paper-saving layouts as well as contact sheets. Use the large range of built in layouts or quickly and easily create your own.

- **Publish to PDF**
  Export your documents to PDF, with powerful options for professional printing (PDF/X-1 compatibility and prepress marks).

- **Powerful Image Export Optimizer**
  The Export Optimizer lets you see how your image will look (and how much space it will take up) *before* you save it! Its multi-window display provides side-by-side WYSIWYG previews of image quality at various output settings, so you can make the best choice every time. Export to a wide range of graphic formats including HD photo and TIF (48- and 64-bit RGB; or 16-bit Greyscale).

Installation

Minimum:

- Windows-based PC with DVD/CD drive and mouse

- Microsoft Windows® XP* SP2 (32 bit), Windows® Vista, or Windows® 7 operating system

- 512MB RAM

- 462MB free hard disk space.

- 1024 x 768 monitor resolution

Additional disk resources and memory are required when editing large and/or complex images.

* Requires Microsoft Windows Imaging Component.

Optional:

- Windows-compatible printer

- TWAIN-compatible scanner and/or digital camera

- Pressure-sensitive pen tablet

- Internet account and connection required for accessing online resources

First-time install

To install PhotoPlus X5 simply insert the PhotoPlus X5 Program disc into your drive. The AutoRun feature automatically starts the Setup process. Just answer the on-screen questions to install the program.

Re-install

To re-install the software or to change the installation at a later date, select **Control Panel** from the Windows Start menu and then click on the **Programs - Uninstall a program** option. Make sure the disc is inserted into your drive, then select Serif PhotoPlus X5, click the **Change** button and simply follow the on-screen instructions.

 Use equivalent options for Windows XP.

2 Getting Started

Startup Wizard

Once PhotoPlus has been installed, you're ready to start!

- The Setup routine during install adds a **Serif PhotoPlus X5** entry to the Windows Start menu. Use the Windows **Start** button to pop up the Start Menu, click on **All Programs** and then click the PhotoPlus item.

On program launch, the Startup Wizard is displayed which offers different routes into PhotoPlus:

- **Start New Image** (or **Start New Animation**) , to start from scratch.

- **Import From Twain**, to acquire images (from scanner or camera).

- **HDR Photo Merge**, for bracketing photos taken at different exposure levels.

- **Open PhotoPlus Organizer**, to manage and filter photos, for PhotoPlus.

- **Open**, lists recently opened photos and PhotoPlus projects. Hover over each entry for a quick preview!

- **Learn**, to access online tutorial resources.

Use the **Choose Workspace** drop-down menu to choose your workspace appearance (i.e., Studio tab positions, tab sizes, and show/hide tab status). You can adopt the default workspace profile **<Default Profile>**, the last used profile **<Current Profile>**, a range of pre-defined profiles, or a custom workspace profile you've previously saved.

> As you click on different profiles from the menu, your workspace will preview each tab layout in turn.

If you don't want to use the Startup Wizard again, check the "Don't show this wizard again" box. However, we suggest you leave it unchecked until you're familiar with the equivalent PhotoPlus commands. Switch the wizard back on again by checking **Use Startup Wizard** via **Preferences...** (General menu option) on the **File** menu.

Starting from scratch

PhotoPlus deals with two basic kinds of image files. We'll differentiate them as **pictures** (still images) and **animations** (moving images). The two types are closely related, and creating either from scratch in PhotoPlus involves the same series of steps.

PhotoPlus lets you create an image based on a pre-defined canvas size (e.g., 10 x 8 in). Different canvas size options are available from a range of categories (International/US Paper, Photo, Video, Web, or Animation). Alternatively, you can create your own custom canvas sizes, and even store them for future use. For either preset or custom sizes, the resolution can be set independently of canvas size.

When you create a new image, you can choose to work in different colour modes, i.e. RGB or Greyscale, in either 8- or 16-bits/channel. Use a **Bit Depth** of 16 bit for higher levels of image detail modes.

To create a new image or animation (using Startup Wizard):

1. The first time you launch PhotoPlus, you'll see the **Startup Wizard**, with a menu of choices. Click **Start New Image** or **Start New Animation**.

2. In the New Image dialog, you can either:

   1. For a **preset** canvas size, select a suitable **Category** from the drop-down list. Categories are named according to how your image or animation is intended to be used, e.g. pick a Photo category for photo-sized canvases.

   2. Pick a canvas **Size** from the drop-down list.
      OR

   - For a custom canvas size, enter your own **Width** and **Height**. If the dimensions are non-standard, the Size drop-down list will be shown as "Custom."

     ▽ For future use, save the custom size with **Add Size...**

   💡 Although you can resize the image **canvas size** (width x height) later, it's usually best to allow some extra canvas area at first.

3. (Optional) Add a **Resolution** for the new image file. Leave the resolution as is unless you're sure a different value is required.

4. (Optional) Select a **Colour Mode**, choosing to operate in RGB or Greyscale mode.

5. (Optional) Select a **Bit Depth** of 16 bits per channel for projects which require higher levels of colour detail. Otherwise a bit depth of 8 bits/channel is used as default.

6. (Optional) Select a background type in the **Background** drop-down list.

   - When painting from scratch, you'll normally choose White.

   - You can also choose Background Colour, to use the current background colour shown on the Colour tab.

   - When creating an animation, Transparent is often called for.

7. When you've made your selections, click **OK**.

To create a new picture or animation (during your session):

1. Click 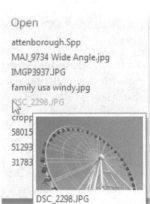 **New** on the **Standard** toolbar. This will open the Startup Wizard (see p. 19) or the New Image dialog (if the Startup Wizard is disabled).

2. In the New Image dialog, set your canvas size (see p. 19) and then check **Animation** to create an animation or leave unchecked for a picture.

3. Click **OK**. The new image or animation opens in a separate untitled window.

Opening an existing file

You can use the Startup Wizard to access files recently viewed in PhotoPlus or any file on your computer. PhotoPlus opens all the standard formats for print and web graphics, in addition to its native SPP format, Adobe Photoshop (PSD) files, and Paint Shop Pro (PSP) files.

Raw files open in a **Raw Studio** environment, which offers image adjustment on the "undeveloped" image before opening. See Opening a raw image on p. 21. Similarly, intermediate HDR images (OpenEXR and Radiance) can be opened in a dialog at any time for readjusting your HDR merge results (see p. 91).

To open a recently opened PhotoPlus Picture or graphic (via Startup Wizard):

1. From the Startup Wizard (at startup time or via **File>New...**), select your SPP file or graphic file from the **Open** section. The most recently opened file will be shown at the top of the list. To see a thumbnail preview of any file before opening, hover over its name in the list.

2. Click the file name to open it.

Open

attenborough.Spp

MAJ_9734 Wide Angle.jpg

IMGP3937.JPG

family usa windy.jpg

DSC_2298.JPG

cropp

58015

51293

31783

DSC_2298.JPG

PhotoPlus opens the image as a maximized currently active document; the document appears in the Documents tab.

> Recently viewed files also appear at the bottom of the **File** menu. Simply select the file name to open it.

To open any image file:

1.   From the Startup Wizard (at startup time or via **File>New...**), click **Open...**.
OR

Click   **Open** on the **Standard** toolbar.

2.   In the Open dialog, select the folder and file name. To open multiple files, press the **Shift** or **Ctrl** key when selecting their names (for adjacent or non-adjacent files).

3.   Click the **Open** button to open the desired image as a maximized document.

To open images by drag-and-drop:

- Drag and drop an image file or preview thumbnail into PhotoPlus from Windows Explorer either:

    - into the current workspace (to create a new layer).
    OR

    - onto the Documents tab (to create a new image window).

Opening a raw image

High-specification SLR digital cameras give the option of saving your photos as JPG, and more recently, as raw files. On some cameras, you may have the best of both worlds, by saving as both simultaneously.

Quite why you would choose one format over the other depends on a host of factors, such as the type of workflow and the level of detail you want to work to. This is best summarized in the following table.

JPG	raw
Basic level of colour or greyscale detail, with 8-bit images	**Highest** level of colour or greyscale detail, with 16-bit images
Small file sizes (so faster write-to-card time)	**Larger** file sizes (so slower write-to-card time)
JPG files are **automatically processed** by camera	raw files are **unprocessed** by camera
Limited adjustment control (post-shoot)	**Absolute** adjustment control (post-shoot)

There is a healthy debate in the photographic industry about which format to choose. Professionally, the old idiom "horses for courses" applies. For example, the need for fast shoot-to-print time (using JPGs) is essential for sports photographers where post-shoot adjustment is not practical. Conversely, a wedding photographer may wish to work with the maximum amount of colour information (using raw images) and then typically make post-shoot adjustments, maintaining flexibility and high detail throughout.

For the amateur or semi-professional photographer, the same factors apply, but format choice may be governed more by quality expectations or cost, rather than "workflow" issues.

Workflow refers to the shoot-to-print progress when working with JPG or raw files. A JPG workflow is destructive, in that your JPG file is "developed" in your camera without user intervention. Conversely, a raw workflow is non-destructive because your raw file is "undeveloped"—you can control your image's development within your photo-editing program (PhotoPlus).

PhotoPlus's **Raw Studio** offers post-shoot adjustments to your raw file **without** affecting the original file. **White balance**, **exposure**, **highlight recovery**, **noise reduction**, and the removal of **chromatic aberration** are all possible. With an in-built histogram, it's easy to firstly check exposure levels and to spot any highlight clipping (suggesting image overexposure), and to secondly make adjustments using the human eye and the histogram in combination.

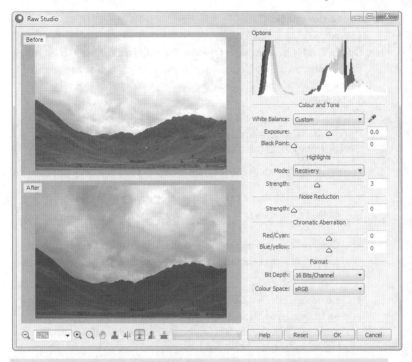

Opening 16-bit HD photos will automatically adopt a 16-bits/channel Colour mode to maintain high-quality colour or tonal detail. modes

Once you click **OK** you won't be able to undo your adjustments—it's therefore recommended to spend time "developing" your image correctly before exiting Raw Studio.

Once you've exited Raw Studio you'll enter the usual PhotoPlus user interface. As for any other file format you can then optionally add text, lines, shapes, and apply some creative filter effects (not all effects are available in 16 bits/channel mode). On saving (**File>Save** or **File>Save As...**), you'll be prompted to save your work as a PhotoPlus picture (.spp) only. Typically most users would then export to a 16-bit file format such as TIF or HDP.

To adjust a raw image:

1. Open a raw file by using [icon] **Open** on the **Standard** toolbar. (see Starting from scratch on p. 18). If opening multiple raw files, once you've adjusted an image, Raw Studio will load the next image automatically until all files are loaded.

> [icon] Open raw images previously copied to your computer, rather than directly from your camera's memory card (e.g., SD).

2. From Raw Studio, adopt the program's, camera's or a custom white balance.

    *   **Auto**: White balance calculated automatically by PhotoPlus. The camera's white balance setting is ignored.

    *   **Camera**: The camera's manual or automatic white balance setting is used. PhotoPlus is not used to set white balance.

    *   **Custom**: Click [icon] **Colour Selector** then hover over a neutral colour on the screen to calculate the white balance manually. Typically, a subject's white shirt or blue sky can be clicked on as the neutral "reference"point.

3. Drag the **Exposure** slider left or right to make the image darker or lighter. The values are equivalent to your camera's f-stop settings, i.e. a value of 1 = 1 f-stop.

> [icon] When increasing the Exposure value, use the histogram to check that your highlights aren't clipped (i.e., when the graph disappears abruptly off the right-hand edge of the histogram).

4. Drag the **Black Point** slider right to set the darkest parts of the image to black (by shifting the histogram's left-most edge, making all "clipped" pixels in the shadow region turn black).

5. For recovery of blown highlights, from the **Mode** drop-down menu choose **Recovery**, and if needed, increase the **Strength** slider until you get ideal results. The **Clip** option, as default, means that highlights remain blown (no recovery is attempted). The **Neutral** option also recovers highlights if you're experiencing colour casting.

6. For Noise reduction set a **Strength**. Noise may be evident on images captured in low light or with a high ISO camera setting. The greater the value, the more smoothing occurs to remove speckling. Too much noise reduction may produce an unwanted blurring effect.

7. Remove unwanted **Chromatic Aberration** (colour fringing on object edges on high-contrast photos) by adjusting **Red/Cyan** or **Blue/Yellow** sliders. Each slider adjusts one colour channel relative to the other channel.

8. To reduce the colour information down to "8 Bits/Channel", select from the **Bit Depth** option. By default, optimum raw colour information is preserved (i.e., 16 Bits/Channel). modes

9. From the **Colour Space** drop-down menu, assign a colour space to your image which matches your intended colour **workspace**. For professional work, AdobeRGB, ProPhoto, or WideGamut offer larger colour spaces (i.e more colours) than the standard RGB (sRGB) space (this is acceptable for most users), but you'll need to enable colour management and pick the same colour space as your chosen workspace. matching

10. Click **OK** (or **Reset** to discard applied adjustments). The raw image becomes your PhotoPlus document.

Getting images from cameras and scanners

If your digital camera or scanner supports the industry-wide **TWAIN** standard, you can bring pictures from these devices directly into PhotoPlus.

To set up your TWAIN device for importing:

-   See the documentation supplied with the device for operating instructions.

To import a TWAIN image:

1. (via Startup Wizard) Choose **Import From Twain**.
    OR
    (During your PhotoPlus session) Choose **Import** from the **File** menu, then select **Acquire**.

2. Complete the procedure using the acquisition dialog associated with the selected TWAIN source.

If you have more than one TWAIN-compatible device installed, you may need to select which source you wish to scan with.

To select a different TWAIN source for scanning:

● Choose **Import** from the **File** menu, then choose **Select Source** from the submenu.

See PhotoPlus Help for some useful tips about scanning.

Saving a file

The process of **saving** differs depending on the type of file you are working on, the file's current saved state and the file type you want to save.

PhotoPlus lets you work on (and save) one of several file types:

● An open **PhotoPlus Picture** (**.spp**) file is project-based and so preserves 'project' information (e.g., layers, masks, paths) when saving the file.

● For a currently open **image** file you can edit and save the image back to its original format. However, if you've added layers, masks, or paths to your image you'll be prompted to optionally create an spp file to preserve 'project' information (otherwise it will be lost). If you choose not to create an spp file, the additional content is included in the now flattened image.

● An intermediate **HDR** image can be saved, which stores the results of an HDR Photo Merge in an HDR file for future use. See Merging bracketed photos for more information.

To save your PhotoPlus Picture (.spp):

● Click the ▦ **Save** button on the **Standard** toolbar.
OR
To save under a different path or base name, choose **Save As...** from the **File** menu. The window title bar is updated accordingly.

> If the current window is untitled or non-native, the Save As dialog opens, and prompts for an SPP file name based on the base name shown in the title bar.

The procedure for an altered image is slightly more complicated as PhotoPlus will assist you in deciding if you want to save or lose any added "project information" added to the original image.

To save your currently open image:

- If you've altered the background layer only and no layers, paths, or masks have been added, you can save (without prompt) the altered image to its current base name (shown in the window title bar) by choosing one of the above **Save** options. Changes are included in the image.
  OR

- If you've added layers, paths, or masks to your image, when you click a **Save** option you'll be asked if you want to preserve the "project" information.

  - In the dialog, click **Yes** to save your project information (as an SPP file).
    OR
    click **No** to save as a flattened image (i.e., without layers).

To revert an image file:

- Click **Revert** from the **File** menu. The last saved version of your image is displayed.

3 Layers & Masks

Basics of using layers

If you're accustomed to thinking of pictures as flat illustrations in books, or as photographic prints, the concept of **image layers** may take some getting used to. In fact, layers are hardly unique to electronic images. The emulsion of photographic film has separate layers, each sensitive to a different colour—and we've all noticed multiple-image depth effects like shop window reflections or mirrored interiors. There is still something magical about being able to build up an image in a series of planes, like sheets of electronic glass, each of which can vary in transparency and interact with the layers below to produce exciting new images and colours.

Kinds of layers

In a typical PhotoPlus image—for example, a photograph you've scanned in, a new picture file you've just created, or a standard bitmap file you've opened— there is one layer that behaves like a conventional "flat" image. This is called the **Background layer**, and you can think of it as having paint overlaid on an opaque, solid colour surface.

You can create any number of new layers in your image. Each new one appears on top of the currently active layer, comprising a stack that you can view and manipulate with the Layers tab. We call these additional layers **standard layers** to differentiate them from the Background layer. Standard layers behave like transparent sheets through which the underlying layers are visible.

In the example above, the standard layers Surfer Girl, Beach, and Sky are arranged foreground to background by their position in the layer stack, with the Background layer not being used.

Other types of layers also exist in PhotoPlus:

- **Shape layers** are specifically designed to keep drawn lines and shapes (including QuickShapes) separate from the other layers so that they remain editable. (See Drawing and editing lines and shapes; p. 154)

- **Text layers**, work like Shape layers, but are intended exclusively for Text. (See Creating and editing text; p. 152)

- **Adjustment layers** apply corrective image adjustments to lower layers. (See Using adjustment layers; p. 56)

- **Filter layers**, are much like standard layers, but you can apply one or more filter effects to the layer without permanently altering layer content. You also have full control over effects in the future. (See Using filter layers; p. 73)

For now though we're concerned mainly with the Background and standard layers.

A key distinction is that pixels on the Background layer are always opaque, while those on standard layers can vary in opacity (or transparency—another way of expressing the same property). That's because standard layers have a "master" Opacity setting that you can change at any time (with on-screen real-time preview), while the Background layer does not. A couple of examples will show how this rule is applied in PhotoPlus:

- Suppose you are creating a new image. The New Image dialog provides three choices for Background: White, Background Colour, and Transparent. If you pick White or Background Colour, the Layers tab shows a single layer in the new image named "Background". If you pick Transparent, however, the single layer is named "Layer 1"—and in this case, the image (typically an animation file) has no Background layer.

- If you cut, delete, or move a selection on the Background layer, the "hole" that's left exposes the current background colour (as shown on the Colour tab). The same operations on a standard layer expose a transparent hole.

Selections and layers

With few exceptions, you will work on just one layer at any given time, clicking in the Layers tab to select the current or **active layer**. Selections and layers are related concepts. Whenever there's a selection, certain tools and commands operate only on the pixels inside the selection—as opposed to a condition where nothing is selected, in which case those functions generally affect the entire active layer.

If your image has multiple layers, and you switch to another layer, the selection doesn't stay on the previous layer—it follows you to the new active layer. This makes sense when you realize that the selection doesn't actually include image content—it just describes a region with boundaries.

Operations involving layers

Many standard operations, such as painting, selecting and moving, Clipboard actions, adjusting colours, applying effects, and so on, are possible on both the Background layer and standard layers.

Others, such as rearranging the order of layers in the stack, setting up different colour interactions (blend modes and blend ranges) between layers, varying layer opacity (transparency), applying 2D layer effects and 3D layer effects, using depth maps, creating animation frames, or masking, only work with standard layers.

Once an image has more than just a background layer, the layer information can only be preserved by saving the image in the native PhotoPlus (.spp) format. Multiple layers are **merged** when you export an image to a standard "flat" bitmap format (e.g., .png). It's best to save your work-in-progress as SPP files, and only export to a different file format as the final step.

Some standard operations can be applied to all layers simultaneously by checking the **Use All Layers** option from the Context toolbar.

To carry out basic layer operations:

- To select a layer, click on its name in the Layers tab. The selected layer is now the **active layer**. Note that each layer's entry includes a preview thumbnail, which is visible at all times and is especially useful when identifying layer contents.

- To select multiple layers together, use **Ctrl**-click or **Shift**-click to select non-adjacent or adjacent layers in the tab's stack. Once selected, multiple layers can be moved, linked, aligned, duplicated, grouped, rearranged, hidden, merged and deleted. To select all standard layers, choose **Select All Layers** from the **Layers** menu, or for just linked layers, choose **Select Linked Layers**.

- To create a new standard layer above the active layer, click the ⊞ **New Layer** button on the Layers tab. Dragging a file icon and dropping it onto the current window also creates a new layer from the dragged image.

- Select 📁 **New Layer Group** to create a group in which you can store layers which have some relationship to each other—some layers may only be related to a specific photo feature such that any changes to those layers will be restricted to the group's scope only. This gives greater control to enable changes to opacity, blend modes and hide/show layer settings for the group rather than for individual layers.

- Click the ◑ **New Adjustment Layer** button to apply an image adjustment to a layer (See Using adjustment layers on p. 56).

- The ▢ **Add Layer Mask** button adds a mask to the currently selected layer.

- The ◠ **Add Layer Depth Map** button creates a depth map for the selected layer.

- The *fx* **Add Layer Effects** button creates a 2D or 3D effect on the layer. Right-click to copy/paste, clear or hide effects.

- To remove one or more selected layers, click the 🗑 **Delete Layer** button on the Layers tab. Hidden layers can also be deleted without prior selection by using **Delete>Hidden Layers**. (You can delete the Background layer, as long as it's not the only layer.)

- 👁 To make a layer's contents visible or invisible, click the **Hide/Show Layer** button next to its name on the Layers tab.

  To view a layer in isolation, press the **Alt** key while clicking on the **Hide/Show Layer** button. All other visible layers are temporarily hidden. Repeat the **Alt**-click procedure to make the temporarily hidden layers visible again.

- Use ▦ 🔒 ✛ 🔒 lock buttons on the Layers tab to prevent accidental modification of opacity, pixel colour, object positions or all three on the active layer (or group), respectively.

- To convert any shape or text layer to a standard layer, right-click on the layer name and choose **Rasterize** from the menu.

- Use different thumbnail sizes in the Layers tab by clicking the ▽ **Tab Menu** button, then choosing **Small Thumbnails** or **Large Thumbnails**.

- To convert the Background layer to a standard (transparent) layer, right-click "Background" on the Layers tab and choose **Promote to Layer**. The layer's name changes from "Background" to "Layer <number>." To convert a standard layer to a Background layer, right-click the layer and choose **Layer to Background**.

- To convert the layer to a non-destructive filter layer, for applying and managing effect and adjustment filters, right-click and select **Convert to Filter Layer**. (See Using filter layers on p. 73)

- To access Layer Properties—including Name, Blend Mode, Opacity, and Blend Ranges—right-click the layer name and choose **Properties...**.

To control layer content:

- To select all layer content use **Select>Select All** or **Ctrl+A**. To select non-transparent regions on a layer, **Ctrl**-click on a layer thumbnail. Use **Invert** to selection transparent regions.

- To move layer content, select one or more layers containing the content to be moved (from the Layers tab), then drag with the **Move Tool** with no selection area present (press **Ctrl+D** to remove any selection).

- To align layer content, select one or more layers (as above), then choose **Align** from the **Layers** menu, then select an option from the submenu.

- To distribute layer content, select one or more layers (as above), then choose **Distribute** from the **Layers** menu, then select an option from the submenu.

To carry out advanced layer operations:

- To create a new standard layer from a selection, choose **New Layer from Selection Copy** or **New Layer from Selection Cut** from the **Layers** menu. The former command leaves the original region intact; the latter cuts the original region to the Clipboard.

- To clone one or more active layers and their contents as new standard layers, right-click the selected layers then choose **Duplicate...** (or **Alt**-drag in the editing window with Move Tool selected). The process also lets you copy the layer to a new or currently opened image.

- To link layers, select multiple layers and choose **Link Layers** from the **Layers** menu (or right-click in the Layers tab).

- To clip a layers contents to the layer below, right-click the layer to be clipped and select **Clip to Layer Below**.

- To rearrange layers, select the layer(s) in the Layers tab and drag up or down. A red line "drop target" appears between layers as you drag. Drop the layer(s) on a target to relocate in the stack.

- To merge layers together into one, right click and choose **Merge Down** (merges into layer below), **Merge Visible** (merges only visible layers), **Merge Selected Layers** (merges currently selected layers), or **Merge All** (to flatten all layers into one).

Using layer groups

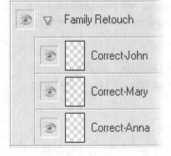

For greater management and efficiency it is possible to place selected layers into a created **group**. There are many reasons why you might want to use groups in addition to layers. Here are a few...

- To create a self-contained group of layers which are all related, e.g. all the Retouch layers used in your photo.

- To collect layers together which make up a specific photo feature, e.g. the beach components of a seaside shot.

- To make a mask or blend apply to only specific layers, i.e. those that contained within a group.

- To apply changes to a group that you would otherwise have to apply to each layer in turn—thus improving efficiency.

In reality a group is really just another layer but one which can store layers within itself. It's not surprising then that a group can have its own blend mode, opacity and blend ranges just like a layer. A group can also be merged and made visible/invisible—or even grouped within another group.

To create a Layer Group:

1. In the Layers tab, select a layer to set the position in the layer stack in which you want to place the Layer Group.

2. Click the ▢ **New Layer Group** button (or select **New Layer Group...** from the **Layers** menu).

3. In the dialog, enter group name, blend mode, opacity, and blend range for the group.

4. Click **OK**.

To add one or more layers to a Layer Group:

- Select the layer(s) you want to add to the group and drag onto the group name (a red line indicates where the layer is to be placed). The layer(s) will then appear indented under the group.

Alternatively, you can select multiple layers and add them to a new unnamed group by selecting either **New Layer Group from Selected Layers** or **Group Layers** on the **Layers** menu.

To remove a layer:

- To remove the layer(s), drag the layer away from the group and drop it into an ungrouped area of the Layers tab. You can also use **Ungroup Layers** from the **Layers** menu if all layers are to be removed.

To merge a Layer Group:

- To flatten the layer group, select the group and choose **Merge>Merge Layer Group** from the **Layers** menu.

You cannot move the Background layer to a group.

Blending control in layer groups

Layers that belong to layer groups automatically "pass through" to other layers as if they were not grouped. This is because a Cross-Fade blend mode is enabled on the layer group when it is created.

Layers within the group behave as if ungrouped, and blend with other lower ungrouped layers. This is especially useful for one or more adjustment layers in a group, where the adjustment layer is active on all layers below it (rather than be "protected" when the blend mode is Normal).

Using blend modes

You can think of **blend modes** as different rules for putting pixels together to create a resulting colour. In PhotoPlus, you'll encounter blend modes in several contexts:

- As a property of individual **tools**, the tool's blend mode determines what happens if you use the tool to apply a new colour pixel on top of an existing colour pixel. Note that once you've applied paint to a region, that's it— you've changed the colour of pixels there. Subsequently changing a tool's blend mode won't alter brush strokes you've already laid down!

Behind and Clear modes are only available for tools and not for layers.

A Crossfade blend mode (not shown) is also available exclusively for layer groups. The blend mode provides **pass-through blending**, i.e. layers within the group behave as if ungrouped, and blend with other lower ungrouped layers. See Blending in layer groups.

- As a property of individual **layers**, a layer's blend mode determines how each pixel on that layer visibly combines with those on layers below. (Because there are no layers below the Background layer, it can't have a blend mode.) Note that changing a layer's blend mode property doesn't actually alter the pixels on the layer—so you can create different blend mode effects after creating the image content, then merge layers when you've achieved the result you want.

- As a property of certain 3D layer effects, where the blend mode is one of many settings that determine a colour change superimposed on the layer's pixels. The effects themselves are editable and don't alter the actual pixel values—nor does the effect's blend mode alter the layer's blend mode setting.

For an illustration of the individual blend modes, see "blend modes" in the PhotoPlus Help's index.

A tool or layer's **Opacity** setting interacts with its blend mode to produce varying results. For details, see Adjusting opacity/transparency on p. 41.

To set a tool's blend mode:

- Select the tool and use the drop-down list (displays Normal by default) on the tool's Context toolbar.

To set a standard layer's blend mode:

- Select the layer and choose the mode from the blend mode's drop-down list.

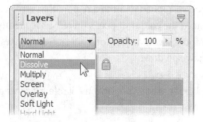

It's also possible to include or exclude tones or colours to be included in any blending operation by using **blend ranges**. For more details, see PhotoPlus Help.

Adjusting opacity/transparency

Varying opacity is rather like lighting a gauze backdrop in a theatre: depending on how light falls on it, it can be rendered either visible or invisible, or in between. Fully opaque pixels contribute their full colour value to the image. Fully transparent pixels are invisible: they contribute nothing to the image. In-between pixels are called semi-transparent.

Fully opaque text (100% Opacity)   *Semi-transparent text (50% Opacity)*

Opacity and **transparency** describe essentially the same thing (like "half full" and "half empty"). They both describe the extent to which a particular pixel's colour contributes to the overall colour at that point in the image.

You'll primarily encounter opacity in one of these two contexts:

- As a property of the pixels laid down by individual **tools** (Paintbrush, Clone, Eraser, Fill, Smudge, QuickShape, and more). When you paint on-screen with one of these tools, you're applying pixels—pixels that are more or less opaque, depending on the tool's opacity setting. Note that once you've applied paint to a region, that's it—you've changed the opacity of pixels there. Subsequently changing a tool's opacity setting won't alter brush strokes you've already laid down!

- As a property of individual **standard layers** (in example above). The layer's opacity setting affects all the pixels on the layer, and is cumulative with the opacity of individual pixels already there.

To set a tool's opacity:

- Select the tool (e.g., Paintbrush Tool) and from the Context toolbar either enter a percentage **Opacity** value directly or use the slider (click the option's right arrow button).

To set a layer's opacity:

- Select the layer in the Layers tab and adjust the **Opacity** setting at the top of the tab—either enter a percentage **Opacity** value directly or use the slider (click the option's right arrow button).

To read the opacity values of pixels on the active layer:

1. Select the ✐ **Colour Pickup Tool** from the **Tools** toolbar and move it around the image.

2. Read the value shown for "O" (Opacity) on the Hintline (e.g., O:40%).

   RGB: 67 255 94 O:60%

   The readout updates constantly, showing the opacity value of each pixel under the cursor.

For more useful hints and tips about using opacity, see PhotoPlus Help.

Using depth maps

Depth maps let you add remarkable 3D realism to ordinary images. A standard "flat" image, of course, has only two dimensions: X and Y, or width and height. Adding a depth map to a layer gives you an extra channel that stores information for a third (Z-axis or depth) dimension, in effect adding "volume" to the image. It's as if the original image acquires a surface with peaks and valleys—and you can play with the elevation of the landscape to achieve different visual results.

The example opposite was created simply by painting in white (on a green background) with a fuzzy brush on the depth map.

Changes on the "map" layer produce the effect of highs and lows in the "surface"... it's like using a 3D brush!

You can also combine depth maps with pre-defined 3D effects hosted in the Instant Effects tab (if you can't see it, switch on via **Window>Studio Tabs**) to create fascinating surfaces and textures—simply click on a thumbnail from one

of the tab's categorized galleries with your layer containing the depth map
selected, e.g.

*Elements -
Fire Storm*

*Abstract -
Plasma*

*Stone -
Polished Stone*

To create a depth map:

1. Select the layer (or group) in the Layers tab and click   **Add Layer
    Depth Map**.

    You'll see a thumbnail of the depth map appear to the right of the bitmap
    thumbnail. The Depth Map is initially selected.

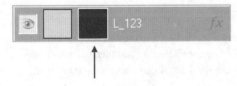

2. Paint directly on your page (you're actually painting or erasing directly on
    the map). Your brush stroke on the depth map produces interesting
    depressions and ridges on the image, which are exposed by 3D lighting
    effects automatically applied from the 3D Effects category.

    The Layers tab shows the brush strokes on the depthmap thumbnail.

While working on the layer, you can switch back and forth between the bitmap,
depth map, and (optional) mask by clicking the appropriate layer thumbnail.

For a layer filled with green pixels:

depthmap selected   *bitmap selected*

You can also switch the depth map off and on to assess its contribution to the image, or subtract it for creative reasons.

To switch the depth map off and on:

- **Shift**-click its preview thumbnail, next to the layer name. When the depth map is switched off a red "X" appears across the thumbnail.

To remove the depth map and cancel its effects on the layer:

- Select the map thumbnail and click the layer tab's 🗑 **Delete** button. (Don't press the **Delete** key!)

Importing a depth map

Another way of incorporating a depth map is to create a suitable bitmap image separately (or borrow one from somewhere else) and then paste it via the Clipboard into an existing PhotoPlus depth map (depthmap thumbnail selected).

Using masks

Masking in a program like PhotoPlus is a bit more complicated than applying masking tape to the screen! But fundamentally the concept is the same: you can hide certain parts of an image—in this case by rendering them transparent, hence invisible. To do that, you create a **mask** on a non-Background layer (the Background layer doesn't support transparency).

By changing the **greyscale** values on the mask (using the paint tools and other devices), you can impose corresponding changes in the **opacity** of the underlying layer's pixels (values stored as the layer's **alpha channel**). For example, by applying a gradient "blacking out" across the mask, you gradually render the layer's underlying pixels transparent, and they disappear from the image (see above).

Besides the creative possibilities, ranging from vignetting to multi-layer montage to gradient-fill masking (see example above) and beyond, a great feature of working on a mask is that it is "temporary". If you don't like the way things are going, you can abandon your changes and start over without ever having affected the actual pixels on the layer!

Each non-Background layer can have one mask at any given time. (The Background layer can't have one because it doesn't support transparency.) Mask information, like layer information, can only be preserved by saving the image in the native PhotoPlus (.spp) format.

Masking can also be applied to adjustment and effect filters, where you can isolate regions (e.g., an image background) to which you want a filter to be applied. (See Using filter masks on p. 76). Similarly, you can use studio-based filter masking on adjustments by using PhotoFix (see p. 68).

Creating the mask

Before you can use a mask, you have to create it on a particular layer. The mask can start out as transparent (revealing the whole layer), opaque (hiding the whole layer), a transparency gradient (opposite) or—if you create it from a selection—a bit of both (with only the selected region hidden or revealed). The mask shows as a mask thumbnail.

The choice depends on how you want to work with the layer's contents. By darkening portions of a clear mask, you can selectively fade layer pixels. By lightening an opaque mask, you selectively reveal layer pixels.

To create a mask:

1.   Select a layer in the Layers tab. This is the layer where you want to create the mask, and select specific region(s) if desired.

2.   Then either:

- Click the [icon] **Add Layer Mask** button to create a Reveal All mask (or Reveal Selection if there is one). Instead, **Alt**-click the button for a Hide All Mask (or Hide Selection).

     OR

- Choose **Mask>Add Mask** from the **Layers** menu and then one of the following from the submenu:
     • **Reveal All** for a transparent mask over the whole layer
     • **Hide All** for an opaque mask over the whole layer
     • **Reveal Selection** for an opaque mask with transparent "holes" over the selected region(s)
     • **Hide Selection** for a transparent mask with opaque "blocks" over the selected region(s)

On the Layers tab, a mask preview thumbnail appears, confirming that a mask exists.

Editing on the mask

When you create your mask you immediately enter Edit Mask mode, where you can use the full range of painting tools, selection options, flood fills, gradient fills, and effects to alter the mask's greyscale values. These manipulations cause corresponding changes in opacity, which in turn changes the appearance of the pixels on the layer itself.

The image window's titlebar shows "**Mask**", indicating that a mask is currently being edited. The Colour tab switches to Greyscale mode when you're editing a mask, and reverts to the previous setting when you exit Edit Mask mode. This means anything you paste from the Clipboard onto the mask will automatically be converted to greyscale.

> As long as you are editing the mask, you're only seeing a preview of changes on the layer.

You can switch out of Edit Mask mode at any time to edit the active layer directly (or any other part of the image), then switch back to resume work on the mask.

To edit the active layer:

- Click the layer thumbnail to the left of the Mask thumbnail. The thumbnail is then bordered in white.

To edit the active layer's mask:

- Click the mask thumbnail, or check **Edit Mask** on the **Layers** menu.

In Edit Mask mode, you're normally viewing not the mask, but rather the effects of changes "as if" you were making them on the layer below. Adding a Reveal All mask can be a bit confusing, because there's initially no evidence the mask is there at all (i.e. the layer appears exactly the same as it did before you added the mask)!

It's sometimes helpful to switch on the **View Mask** setting, which hides the layer and lets you see **only** the mask, in all its greyscale glory. For example, a Reveal All mask appears pure white in View Mask mode—the white represents a clear mask with no effect on the underlying layer pixels' opacity. View Mask can also be useful in the latter stages of working on a mask, to locate any small regions that may have escaped your attention.

To view the active layer's mask:

- **Alt**-click the mask preview thumbnail. **Alt**-click again to stop viewing the mask.

White or light portions of the mask reveal layer pixels (make them more opaque). Black or dark portions hide layer pixels (making them more transparent).

You can **disable** the mask to see how the layer looks without the mask's effects. Note that disabling the mask is not the same as cancelling Edit Mask mode—it only affects your view of the layer, not which plane (i.e. mask or layer) you're working on.

To disable the active layer's mask:

Shift-click the mask preview thumbnail or right-click it and select **Disable Mask** (or select from the **Layers>Mask**). (**Shift**-click again or uncheck the menu item to enable masking again.)

When the mask is disabled, a red "X" appears across its thumbnail.

If you want to fine-tune a mask or layer's position independently of each other it's possible to **unlink** them. You may have noticed a small link button between the layer and mask thumbnails on the Layers tab, i.e.

A click on this button will unlink the layer and mask, changing the button to display a red cross through it ( ); you can also right click the mask preview thumbnail to link/unlink. By selecting the layer or mask thumbnail, you can then drag the layer or mask on the page, respectively. After fine-tuning, click the button to relink the mask to the layer.

Masks and selections

Suffice it to say that a selection, which lets you isolate specific parts of the active layer, often makes an ideal basis for a mask. Once you've created, modified, and manipulated a selection, it's easy to turn it into a mask.

To create a mask from a selection:

1. Choose **Mask>Add Mask** from the **Layers** menu. Remember you can't create a mask on a background layer!

2. To create a mask revealing the selected region, choose **Reveal Selection** from the submenu. Pixels outside the selection will be 100% masked.
    OR
    To create a mask hiding the selected region, choose **Hide Selection** from the submenu. Pixels outside the selection will be revealed.

You can also select part of an image to create a custom brush shape, for example a textured brush or special shape.

Conversely, you can **create a selection** directly from the mask. Within the resulting selection, pixels that are lighter on the mask (conferring more opacity) become relatively more selected. This correlates with Paint to Select mode (see p. 107), where painting in lighter tones also confers "selectedness."

To create a selection from a mask:

*   **Ctrl**-click on the layer's mask thumbnail, or select the mask preview thumbnail and choose **Create from Mask** from the **Select** menu.

In the selection that results, darker areas on the mask become relatively less selected than lighter areas, i.e. more protected from changes.

4 Image Adjustments & Effects

Introduction to image adjustments

A major part of photo-editing is making corrections (i.e., **adjustments**) to your own near-perfect images. Whether you've been snapping with your digital camera or you've just scanned a photograph, at some point you may need to call on PhotoPlus's powerful photo-correction tools to fix some unforeseen problems.

For photo-correction, several methods can be adopted. You can use a combination of:

- **Image colour adjustments**: For applying colour adjustments to a selection or layers.

- **PhotoFix**: For making cumulative corrective adjustments from within a studio environment.

- **Retouch** brush-based tools: Red Eye, Smudge, Blur, Sharpen, Dodge/Burn (for exposure control), Sponge (for saturation control), Scratch Remover.

If you work with raw images you can make image adjustments on your unprocessed raw file (before interpolation). Adjustments include **white balance**, **exposure**, **highlight recovery**, **noise reduction**, and **chromatic aberration** removal. See Opening a raw image on p. 21.

Overview: Adjusting image colours

PhotoPlus provides a number of different adjustment filters that you can apply to a selection or to an active standard layer. Typically, these adjustments are used to correct deficiencies in the original image.

Each adjustment can be applied in one of several ways:

- via the **Adjustments tab**, as an **Adjustment Layer**. (Non-destructive).

- via **PhotoFix**, a studio environment for managing and applying cumulative adjustments. (Non-destructive).

- via **Image>Adjust**, on a Filter Layer. (Non-destructive).

- via **Image>Adjust**, on a standard layer. (Destructive).

Here's a summary of the available PhotoPlus image adjustments.

- **Levels**: Displays a histogram plot of lightness values in the image, from which you can adjust the tonal range by shifting dark, light, and gamma values.

- **Curves**: Displays lightness values in the image using a line graph, and lets you adjust points along the curve to fine-tune the tonal range.

- **Brightness/Contrast**: Brightness refers to overall lightness or darkness, while contrast describes the tonal range, or spread between lightest and darkest values.

- **Shadow/Highlight/Midtone**: Controls the extent of shadows, highlights, and contrast within the image.

- **Hue/Saturation/Lightness**: Hue refers to the colour's tint—what most of us think of as rainbow or spectrum colours with name associations, like "blue" or "magenta". Saturation describes the colour's purity—a totally unsaturated image has only greys. Lightness is what we intuitively understand as relative darkness or lightness—ranging from full black at one end to full white at the other.

- **Colourize**: Lets you recolour an image using Hue, Saturation, and Lightness.

- **Vibrance**: Boosts low-saturation colours in your image, while high-saturation colours are less affected.

- **Colour Balance**: Lets you adjust colour and tonal balance for general colour correction in the image.

- **Replace Colour**: Tags one or more ranges of the full colour spectrum that require adjustment in the image, then apply variations in hue, saturation, and/or brightness to just those colour regions (not to be confused with the simpler Replace Colour Tool).

- **Selective Colour**: Lets you add or subtract a certain percentage of cyan, magenta, yellow, and/or black ink for creating effects.

- **Channel Mixer** Modifies a colour channel using a mix of the current colour channels.

- **Gradient Map**: Lets you remap greyscale (lightness) information in the image to a selected gradient. The function replaces pixels of a given lightness in the original image with the corresponding colour value from the gradient spectrum.

- **Lens Filter**: Adjusts the colour balance for warming or cooling down your photos. It digitally mimics the placement of a filter on the front of your camera lens.

- **Black and White Film**: Used for greyscale conversion with controllable source channel input.

- **Threshold**: Creates a monochromatic (black and white) rendering. You can set the threshold, i.e. the lightness or grey value above which colours are inverted.

- **Equalize**: Evenly distributes the lightness levels between existing bottom (darkest) and top (lightest) values.

- **Negative Image**: Inverts the colours, giving the effect of a photographic negative.

- **Clarity**: Lets you sharpen up your photos using local contrast.

- **Posterize**: Produces a special effect by reducing the image to a limited number of colours.

Instead of the manual tonal adjustments above, the PhotoPlus **Image** menu affords a number of functions you can apply to correct shadow/highlight values in an image automatically. **Adjust>AutoLevels** or **Adjust>AutoContrast** may do the job in one go; if not, you can use **Adjust>Levels...** or **Adjust>Shadow/Highlight/Midtone...**.

Use the Histogram tab to display statistics and image colour values, helping you to evaluate the kinds of image adjustments that may be needed.

Using adjustment layers

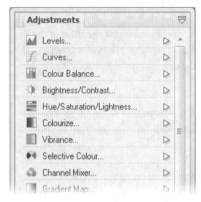

Adjustment layers are recommended for applying image adjustments experimentally and non-destructively to your image.

An adjustment layer is created by selecting an adjustment from the **Adjustments tab**. As its name suggests, an adjustment layer is considered a layer so it will appear in the Layers tab on creation.

The Adjustments tab lists available adjustments in a selectable adjustments list; after selection, the tab displays a Settings pane for that adjustment (and for any selected adjustment layer present in the Layers tab).

Unlike the other layer types, adjustment layers don't store content in the form of bitmap images, text, or shapes. Rather, an adjustment layer applies the adjustment to content on **all** layers below it (although you can restrict the effects of the adjustment by adding to a group or by clipping to the immediate layer below).

The layer is essentially a container in which only the adjustment's settings and its layer properties are stored.

You can drag an adjustment layer up or down within the list to determine exactly which other layers are below and therefore affected by it.

Adjustment layers let you revisit the settings for a given adjustment as often as needed, while continuing to edit the image in other ways. If you later decide you don't even need an adjustment, you can simply remove it!

The following adjustments are available:

- **Levels:** Adjust contrast and tonal range by shifting dark, light, and mid-tone values.

- **Curves:** Fine-tune lightness (luminance) values in the image or colour channel using a line graph.

- **Colour Balance:** Adjust colour and tonal balance for general colour correction in the image.

- **Brightness/Contrast:** Vary brightness and/or contrast.

- **Hue/Saturation/Lightness:** Vary hue, saturation, and/or lightness values.

- **Colourize**: Vary hue, saturation, and/or lightness to colourize an image.

- **Vibrance**: Boosts the saturation of low-saturation colours (while limiting saturation of already saturated colours).

- **Selective Colour:** Add or subtract a certain percentage of cyan, magenta, yellow, and/or black ink.

- **Channel Mixer:** Modify a colour channel using a mix of the current colour channels.

- **Gradient Map:** Remap greyscale (lightness) information in the image to a selected gradient.

- **Lens Filter**: Apply a colour filter to warm up (or cool down) your image.

- **Black & White Film**: Convert your colour image to black and white intelligently.

- **Threshold Filter:** Create a monochromatic (black and white) representation.

- **Posterize:** Apply the Posterize effect by limiting the number of lightness levels.

- **Negative Image:** Invert each colour, replacing it with an "opposite" value.

For more in-depth details on each adjustment, view the PhotoPlus Help, click the Contents tab, and open the "Making Image Adjustments" book.

To create an adjustment layer:

1. From the Adjustments tab, select an adjustment. Click ▷ to choose a default adjustment or a named preset by expanding the adjustment entry.

2. In the Layers tab, the new adjustment layer is inserted above the active layer. The adjustment is applied to all underlying layers.

3. From the Adjustments tab, change the applied adjustment layer's settings to suit your requirements. For example, for a levels adjustment, you can drag the histogram pointers to alter levels.

 Just like other layer types (standard, Text, Shape, Filter, but not Background), adjustment layers can have a mask applied to them. By default, a mask thumbnail is shown on the adjustment layer. Select this to apply a mask to your adjustment layer. (See Using masks.)

To save an adjustment layer as a new preset:

1. Select and then modify an adjustment layer in the Adjustments tab.

2. Click ⊞ **Add Preset**.

3. From the dialog, name your custom adjustment layer, and click **OK**.

Custom adjustments will appear under the adjustment's type in the tab's adjustment list.

To modify an adjustment layer:

1. Click the adjustment layer's name in the Layers tab.

2. From the Adjustments tab, modify the applied adjustment layer's settings.

To hide/show an adjustment layer:

*   Click **Hide/Show Layer** on the Layers tab.

To delete an adjustment layer:

*   (via Layers tab) Select the adjustment layer and click **Delete Layer**.

    OR

*   (via Adjustments tab) with the adjustment's settings pane showing, click **Delete Layer**. This removes the currently selected adjustment layer, so be careful not to remove additional adjustment layers in the Layers tab by clicking multiple times.

To reset an adjustment layer:

1. Click the adjustment layer's name in the Layers tab.

2. From the Adjustments tab, select **Restore Default Settings**.

To access layer properties for an adjustment layer:

*   Right-click the layer name and choose **Properties...**.

As with other layers, you can change the adjustment layer's name, set its opacity, blend mode, and/or blend ranges.

Clipping adjustment layers

Clipping allows you to restrict the scope of an **adjustment layer**, i.e. the adjustment influences **only** the layer immediately below it, rather than all underlying layers.

To clip an adjustment layer:

- Click ⊡ **Clip to Layer Below** on the selected adjustment layer (in the Adjustments tab).

You'll see your adjustment layer become indented, indicating that it is clipped to the layer below. The circled icon indicates a clipped layer.

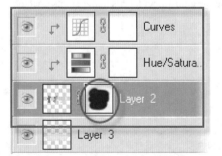

To unclip a selected layer:

- In the Adjustments tab, click ⊡ **Clip to Layer Below**.

One additional benefit of the clipping feature is that you apply the mask on the lower layer (thumbnail circled below) to multiple adjustment layers that are "clipped" to that lower layer. This saves you creating a mask per adjustment layer.

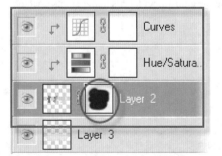

Retouching

The **Tools** toolbar includes an assortment of comparatively simple pressure-sensitive brush-based tools that come in handy at various stages of photo editing. Retouching tools work on Background and standard layers, but not on text layers or shape layers.

On the **Retouch Tools** flyout:

Red Eye Tool - for correcting the "red eye" phenomenon common in colour snapshots

Smudge Tool - for picking up colour from the click point and "pushing" it in the brush stroke direction

Blur Tool - for reducing contrast under the brush, softening edges without smearing colours

Sharpen Tool - for increasing contrast under the brush, enhancing apparent sharpness

Dodge Tool - for lightening an area

Burn Tool - for darkening an area

Sponge Tool - for increasing or decreasing the colour saturation under the brush

Replace Colour Tool - for swapping one colour for another

On the **Blemish Tools** flyout:

Blemish Remover - for intelligently painting out skin blemishes

Scratch Remover - for filling in small gaps or dropouts in an image

Patch Tool - for painting out selected areas

Straightening a photo

As an image adjustment, the **Straighten Tool** can be used to align a crooked image back to horizontal (e.g., restoring proper horizontal alignment in a scanned image that wasn't aligned correctly on the scanner). Use the tool to trace a new horizon against a line in the image—the image automatically orients itself to the drawn horizon.

Before *After*
(horizon line drawn by dragging)

You can straighten using one of two methods: As a separate tool used directly on your image (below) or via the PhotoFix studio environment (see p. 63).

To straighten (via Straighten Tool):

1. Choose the ![icon] **Straighten Tool** from the ![icon] **Crop Tools** flyout on the **Tools** Toolbar.

2. On the Context toolbar, choose an option from the **Canvas** drop-down list. This lets you decide how your straightened image will be displayed:

    •   **Crop** - Crops and adjusts the straightened image so that it displays on the largest possible canvas size, without displaying any border.

    •   **Expand to Fit** - Increases the canvas size to display the entire straightened image. The border area is filled with the current background colour.

    •   **Original Size** - Displays the straightened image within the original canvas dimensions. The border area is filled with the current background colour.

On the image that needs straightening, look for a straight line on the image to which you can set the new horizon (e.g., the divide between the land and sea above).

3. (Optional) Uncheck **Rotate All Layers** to restrict the operation to the active layer only. Otherwise all layers are rotated.

4. Using the Straighten cursor, drag a horizon from one end of the image's line to the other (the length of the horizon is not important) then release. The image orients itself to the new line.

Using PhotoFix

PhotoFix provides an image **adjustment** environment within PhotoPlus which simplifies the often complicated process of image correction. The studio environment offers the following key features:

- **Adjustment filters**
  Apply tonal, colour, lens, and sharpening filters.

- **Retouching filters**
  Apply red-eye correction, spot repair, straightening, and cropping.

- **Non-destructive operation**
  All filters are applied without affecting the original picture (by automatically creating a filter layer), and can be edited at any point in the future.

- **Powerful filter combinations**
  Create combinations of mixed adjustment filters for savable workflows.

- **Selective masking**
  Apply filters to selected regions using masks.

- **Save and manage favourites**
  Save filter combinations to a handy **Favourites tab**.

- **Viewing controls**
  Compare before-and-after previews, with tiled- and split-screen controls
  (horizontally and vertically). Use pan and zoom control for moving around
  your picture.

To launch PhotoFix:

- Click 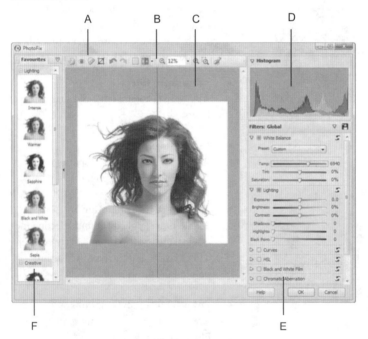 **PhotoFix** on the Photo Studio toolbar.

Let's get familiar with the PhotoFix interface showing a non-default **Split
horizontal** view.

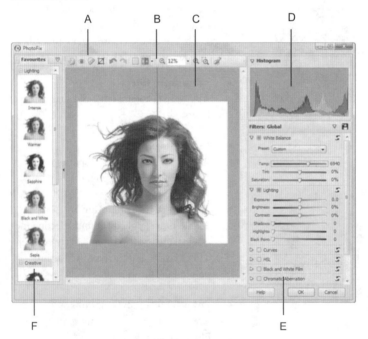

*(**A**) Retouch tools, (**B**) Main toolbar, (**C**) Main Workspace, (**D**) Histogram,
(**E**) Filters, (**F**) Favourites.*

Adjustments overview

Adjustments are made available to the right of the main window from the **Filters** section. Here's a quick overview of all the adjustments hosted in PhotoFix, some tool-based and some available as filters.

Retouch tools:

- **Red Eye**
  Removes the dreaded red eye effect from subject's eyes—commonly encountered with flash photography.

- **Spot Repair**
  Removes skin blemishes and other flaws.

- **Crop**
  Retains a print-size portion of your image while discarding the remainder. Great for home printing, then framing. Optionally, size an unconstrained selection area to crop.

- **Straighten**
  Re-aligns slightly or wildly crooked photos by resetting the image's horizon, then applying an auto-crop.

See supporting PhotoFix Help for more details.

Filter-based:

- **White Balance**
  "Cool down" or "warm up" your photo by adjusting lighting either by selecting presets or customizing temperature/tint combinations.

- **Lighting**
  Simple adjustments to a photo's exposure, brightness, contrast, shadows, and highlights.

- **Curves**
  Correct the tonal range of a photo, i.e. the shadow, midtone, and highlight regions—and control individual colour components.

- **HSL**
  Adjust the Hue, Saturation, and Lightness of your image independently.

- **Black and White Film**
  Intelligently apply greyscale by varying the grey tones of red, green or blue colours in your original image. Also apply colour tints.

- **Chromatic Aberration**
  Reduces red/cyan or blue/yellow fringing on object edges.

- **Lens Distortion**
  Fixes barrelling and pincushion distortion encountered when photographing straight-edged objects at close range.

- **Lens Vignette**
  Removes darkening in photo corners.

- **Unsharp Mask**
  Makes your image sharper at image edges—great for improving image quality after other adjustments have been made.

Some adjustments can also be applied independently from the **Effects** menu.

To apply an adjustment (from a favourites preset):

1. From the **Favourites tab**, scroll the tab to review the categorized adjustments; select a preset or custom thumbnail.

2. Click **OK**.

When applied, your image layer is **automatically** converted to a non-destructive filter layer with a PhotoFix adjustment entry nested under the filter layer entry.

To apply an adjustment (using custom settings):

1. Review the available adjustments in the Filters section, before expanding the adjustment you want to apply by clicking **Expand filter.**

2. Modify the adjustment using sliders, check boxes, graph adjustments, and drop-down menus (you can also enter absolute values into available input boxes). The image will be adjusted automatically to reflect the new settings in the preview window.

   You'll notice the adjustment filter is enabled once a setting is changed, i.e. the **Enable/disable filter** option becomes greyed out.

3. Click **OK**. A filter layer is created (as above).

To reset (and disable) a modified adjustment:

- Click **Reset settings** in the top-right corner of the adjustment's pane.

To edit PhotoFix adjustments:

- Double-click the PhotoFix entry on the filter layer. PhotoFix is launched with the previously set adjustments still applied.

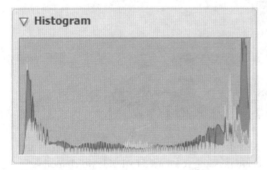

Using PhotoFix masks

Masks in PhotoFix adopt the same principles as layer masks (see p. 45). In PhotoFix however, masking is used to apply adjustment filters to selected "painted" regions of your image or to protect painted regions from change. Painting is used exclusively to create PhotoFix masks.

Each new mask comprises the selected mask region, plus a set of adjustments applied to that mask. You can change the adjustments associated with the mask at a later date.

In the first example below, the model's hair has been masked by painting, allowing White Balance to be adjusted in that painted region only. Conversely, in the second example, the sky has been painted to protect it from masking, allowing light levels to be adjusted for Tower Bridge's stonework.

To achieve the above, PhotoFix uses two mask modes, namely **Mode Select** and **Mode Protect**. When you begin masking you'll need to decide which mode you want to use.

To apply a mask:

1. Select **Create Mask** from the main toolbar.

2. In the Mask Brush pane, select the **Add Region** tool.

Mask Brush	↺
![] Mode: Select ▼	

3. Adjust the settings to suit your requirements. For example, adjust Brush Size to paint larger or more intricate regions.

4. In the **Mode** drop-down menu, choose one of the following options:

   • **Select**: Choose this if you want to apply the filter only to the regions you paint. This is the default setting.

   • **Protect**: Choose this if you want to apply the filter to all areas, except for those that you paint.

5. Using the brush cursor, paint the regions to be masked (selected areas are painted in green; protected areas in red).

6. Click **Accept**.

7. Apply your adjustments as described previously, which will make a change to your masked regions.

Adding multiple masks

So far we've looked at an individual mask applied to an image. However, PhotoFix also supports multiple masks where a different set of adjustments can be applied to each mask. You can therefore build up a patchwork of masked regions for absolute and selective control of image adjustments.

To apply additional masks:

1. In PhotoFix, click the down arrow on the Filters heading.

Filters: Global   ▽ 💾

2. From the drop-down list, select **New...**.

3. In the Mask Brush pane, change settings and paint as described previously in "To apply a mask".

4. Click **OK**. The new mask, named Mask 1, Mask 2, etc. is applied to your image.

5. Apply your adjustments as described previously.

6. Repeat the process for further masks.

Once applied, masks are applied cumulatively. The default global mask is applied to your image first, then Mask 1, then Mask 2, etc., if present. As a result, you may wish to rearrange the mask order for different results. You can also rename and delete masks.

To rearrange, rename or delete a mask:

1. From the down arrow on the Filters heading, select **Manage...**.

2. From the dialog, select a mask and use appropriate supporting buttons.

3. Click **OK**.

To edit a mask:

1. From the down arrow on the Filters heading, select your mask name (a check indicates selection).

2. Modify your adjustments as described previously.

Saving favourites

If there's a specific filter setting (or combination of filters) you want to keep for future use it's easy to save it as a **favourite**. PhotoFix stores preset and custom favourites together in the Favourites tab. You can even create your own categories (e.g., MyAdjusts) within the tab for storing your custom adjustments.

To save a filter(s) as a new favourite:

1. Click **Save Filter** on the modified filter's pane.

2. From the dialog, enter a favourite name and pick a category to save the filter to.

    Optionally, click to save to a new category.

If you want to further manage your favourites into user-defined categories, click **Manage Favourites...** on the **Favourites tab's** Tab Menu.

When increasing the Exposure value, use the histogram to check that your highlights aren't clipped (i.e., when the graph disappears abruptly off the right-hand edge of the histogram).

Overview: Applying special effects

Special effects are grouped into different categories, i.e. **distort**, **blur**, **sharpen**, **edge**, **noise**, **render**, **stylistic**, and **artistic**, which offer you a diverse choice of creative opportunities in PhotoPlus.

Before going ahead and applying your effects, it's a good idea to review Using filter layers (see p. 73) before deciding on your approach, i.e. whether you work non-destructively or destructively.

Each effect can be applied in one of several ways:

- via dialog, on a filter layer (Non-destructive).

- via the Filter Gallery on a filter layer (Non-destructive).

- via dialog, on a standard layer (Destructive).

Equally dramatic effects can be applied by using Warp tools on the Tools toolbar's flyout or 2D/3D layer effects via the Layers tab.

As with image adjustments (see Overview: adjusting image colours on p. 53), you can use filter effects to improve the image, for example by sharpening, but more often the emphasis here is on the "creative" possibilities when effects are applied.

Using filter layers

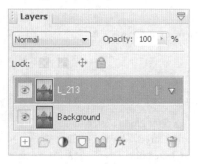

If you apply a filter effect to a standard or background layer, the layer is permanently altered. However, if you want the flexibility of being able to edit your filters at any point in the future (and don't want to destroy the layer contents) you can **convert** your standard or background layer to a **Filter Layer** (e.g., L_213).

Think of a Filter Layer as a way of keeping layer content independent of any filters you wish to use, with the flexibility of being able to manipulate a filter layer in the same way as other layers. Otherwise without filter layers, you would have to repeatedly undo your operations if you've had a rethink and no longer want to apply a specific filter.

When applied, filters are created within **filter groups**, nested individually under the Filter Layer. When you double-click a filter you display its specific settings. You can apply a blend mode and opacity to each filter, and additionally filter masking to the filter group.

> For added security, it's good practice to create a duplicate of any background layer you initially have.

To convert to a filter layer:

- In the Layers tab, right-click a standard or Background layer and choose **Convert to Filter Layer**.

   The layer now shows the letter "F" indicating that it is now a filter layer, and ready to have a filter applied.

To add filters to the filter layer:

1. Select the filter layer.

2. Add an adjustment via the **Image** menu on p. 53.

    OR

    Add an effect via the **Effects** menu or via the Filter Gallery on p. 79.

Each filter, as it is applied, is created within a filter group nested under the selected filter layer. In the example below, the Curves adjustment filter and Gaussian Blur effect filter is applied to the selected filter layer L_213. They'll be stored within Filter Group 1.

As a filter layer has all the properties of standard and Background layers, you may wish to review Basics of using layers (p. 29) and Manipulating layers in PhotoPlus Help. Essentially, you can edit, hide/show, and delete filter layers as for image layers, as well as apply a blend mode or opacity level.

To edit filter layer properties:

*   In the Layers tab, right-click the filter layer and choose **Properties...**.

Managing filter groups and specific filters

When you apply a filter to a filter layer it automatically creates a **filter group**. This allows you to store and manage a selection of filters more easily—you'll be able to control multiple filters in bulk by operating at the group level, e.g. to hide/show, delete, apply blend modes, and opacity to all filters simultaneously. Most operations can be applied equally to group or specific filter, except for masking, which can be used on filter groups but not on individual filters.

To hide/show a filter group/filter:

- Click the **Hide/Show Filter** button next to its name on the Layers tab.

  OR

  Right-click the filter and select **Disable Filter** (or **Enable Filter**).
  OR

  Right-click the filter group and select **Disable Filter Group** (or **Enable Filter Group**).

To delete a filter group/filter:

- Right-click the filter (or filter group) and select **Delete Filter (Group)**.

To create an empty filter group:

Right-click a filter layer and select **Add Filter Group** from the flyout menu.

Just as layers can adopt different blend mode and opacity levels the same is true of filter groups and individual filters. For a refresh on these concepts, see Using blend modes and Adjusting opacity/transparency on p. 39 and p. 41, respectively.

You can use the Blend Options dialog to make blend mode and opacity changes with a dynamic preview, updating as you make change.

To apply a blend mode:

1. Right-click the filter group (or filter) and select **Blend Options...**.

2. From the dialog, select an option from the **Blend Mode** drop-down list.

3. Click **OK**.

To change opacity:

- From the above dialog, enter an **Opacity** level.

Editing filters

The core objective of filter layers is to host filters applied to your image. Once a filter is applied, it's likely that you may want to edit it at a later date.

To edit a filter:

1.   Double-click the filter entry, e.g. Gaussian Blur.

     OR

     Right-click the filter and select **Edit Filter...**.

2.   The filter can then be edited via dialog or Filter Gallery. Adjust the filter and click **OK**.

Using filter masks

In an identical way to layer masks (see p. 45) you can apply a **mask** to a filter layer. However, masks can additionally be used for selective filter control for image correction or artistic reasons. These are called **filter masks**, which limit the influence of any applied filter(s) to that masked region only. Filter masks are applied either automatically (from a selection existing before applying a filter) or manually (after you've applied the filter) to a **filter group** (but never to an individual filter).

See Using layer masks (see p. 45) for more details on masking and masking controls.

To create a filter mask (from a selection):

1. Make a selection on which your mask will be based, e.g. a brush selection around the subject of interest. By default the area outside the selection is masked (i.e. not affected by the filter), while the selection area retains the applied filter. If you want to do the opposite, choose Invert from the **Select** menu.

2. In the Layers tab, select the filter layer to which you wish to apply a filter.

3. Add an adjustment via the **Image** menu.

   OR

   Add an effect via the **Effects** menu or via the Filter Gallery.

   The filter is created within an automatically created filter group, which applies a mask automatically.

4. (Optional) Fine-tune the filter by double-clicking the filter entry and editing the settings.

To create a filter mask (by mask painting):

1. With no selections present, in the Layers tab, select the filter layer to which you wish to apply a filter.

2. Add an adjustment via the **Image** menu.

   OR

   Add an effect via the **Effects** menu or via the Filter Gallery.

3. Right-click the created filter group and select **Add Mask** from the flyout menu and then one of the following from the submenu:

   - **Reveal All** for a transparent mask

   - **Hide All** for an opaque mask.

   A mask thumbnail appears to the left of the filter name.

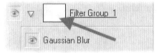

4. Paint or draw on your image using a suitable greyscale value set as your foreground colour tab. The mask thumbnail updates accordingly.

The mask thumbnail (above) would apply a mask which produces a vignette effect. As you can also paint with different greyscale levels you can achieve even more complex masking effects.

To disable (enable) a mask:

- Right-click the filter group and select **Disable Mask** (or **Enable Mask**) from the flyout menu.

To delete a mask:

- Right-click the filter group and select **Delete Mask** from the flyout menu.

Using the Filter Gallery

The Filter Gallery offers a one-stop studio environment for applying **single** or **multiple** filter effects. The gallery hosts sets of filter thumbnails which are categorized into different effect categories (e.g., Distort, Blur, Sharpen, Edge, Artistic, Noise, Render, etc.). Thumbnails are shown in expandable categories.

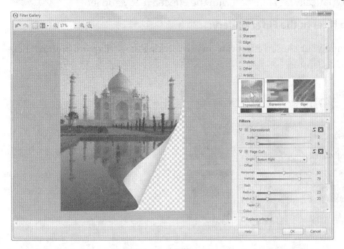

The Filter Gallery offers the following key features:

- Application of individual or multiple filter effects simultaneously.

- Preview window with zoom and pan support.

- Optional **Before** and **After** views arranged as tiles or split-screen, both horizontally and vertically.

You can apply filters via the Filter Gallery in one of two ways:

- permanently to a standard layer.

  OR

  on a Filter Layer (see p. 73), allowing you to protect your image layer, as well as manage your filters at a later date.

To view the Filter Gallery:

- Click  **Filter Gallery** on the Photo Studio toolbar.

> For some effects hosted on the **Effects** menu, the Filter Gallery will automatically be launched with the effect already applied.

To add a filter in the Filter Gallery:

1. Expand your chosen effect category by clicking the ⊞ **Expand** button (click ⊟ to collapse).

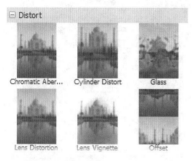

2. Click on an effect thumbnail to apply it to your image.

The applied filter is shown in a **Filters** stack in the lower-right corner of the Filter Gallery. The properties of any selected effect will be displayed in the expanded area under the effect name—you can alter and experiment with these at any time. The filter shows on a light background to indicate selection.

Use the **Undo** button to undo recent changes to the filter (or the **Redo** button to re-apply the changes).

3. Adjust sliders (or enter input values) until your filter suits your requirements. Some filters offer check boxes, drop-down menus, and additional controls (e.g., Advanced settings). The large preview window updates automatically as you adjust any values.

With the **Replace selected** option checked (default), adding a new filter will replace any selected filter in your filter stack.

To add multiple filters:

- Uncheck **Replace selected**, then add one or more additional effects as described above.

Any filter can be temporarily disabled, reset, or deleted once applied.

To disable:

- Click , then click to enable again.

To reset:

- Click . Any changes to settings are reverted back to the filter's defaults.

To delete:

- Click . The filter is removed from the stack.

The effect's properties are expanded by default but can be collapsed to make more of the Filters stack visible.

To collapse/expand filter properties:

- To collapse, click the $\triangledown$ button preceding the filter effect name.

  To expand again, click the $\triangleright$ button.

To replace a filter:

1. Ensure **Replace selected** is checked.

2. Select the filter you wish to replace by clicking anywhere in the filter's pane. On selection, the selected filter shows a lighter background, e.g, Gaussian below.

3. Select a replacement filter from an effect category. Your selected filter is replaced in the stack with no change made to the existing stack order.

The order in which effects appear in the effect list may produce very different results. If you're not happy with the current order, PhotoPlus lets you drag and drop your effects into any position in the stack. Effects are applied in the same way that layers are applied, i.e. the most recently added filter always appears at the bottom of the list and is applied to the picture last (after the other filters above it).

Filters can be moved around the filter list to change the order in which they are applied to the photo.

To reorder filters:

- Drag and drop your filter into any position in the stack. A dotted line indicates the new position in which the entry will be placed on mouse release.

Applying 2D layer effects

Layer effects can be applied to the contents of standard (transparent) layers, text layers, or shape layers. Standard or "2D" layer effects like shadow, glow, bevel, and emboss are particularly well adapted to text, while 3D layer effects (covered elsewhere; p. 85) create the impression of a textured surface.

Unlike image adjustments and **Effects** menu manipulations, layer effects don't directly change image pixels—they work like mathematical "lenses" that transform how a layer's bitmap appears. Since the settings are independent, you can adjust them ad infinitum until you get the result you want!

Here's an example of each effect applied to the letter "A".

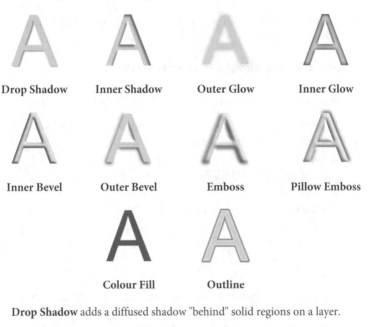

| Drop Shadow | Inner Shadow | Outer Glow | Inner Glow |

| Inner Bevel | Outer Bevel | Emboss | Pillow Emboss |

| Colour Fill | Outline |

- **Drop Shadow** adds a diffused shadow "behind" solid regions on a layer.

- **Inner Shadow** adds a diffused shadow effect inside the edge of an object.

- **Outer Glow** adds a colour border outside the edge of an object.

- **Inner Glow** adds a colour border inside the edge of an object.

- Bevel and Emboss/**Inner Bevel** adds a rounded-edge effect inside an object.

- Bevel and Emboss/**Outer Bevel** adds a rounded-edge effect (resembling a drop shadow) outside an object.

- Bevel and Emboss/**Emboss** adds a convex rounded edge and shadow effect to an object.

- Bevel and Emboss/**Pillow Emboss** adds a concave rounded edge and shadow effect to an object.

- **Colour Fill** lets you apply a specific colour to a layer.

- **Outline** applies a border effect to the edge of an object. See Creating outlines on p. 161.

To apply a shadow, glow, bevel, or emboss effect:

1. From the Layers tab, select a layer and click  **Add Layer Effects**.

2. In the dialog, apply an effect by checking its check box in the list at left. You can apply multiple effects to the layer.

    ✔ Drop Shadow
    Inner Shadow
    Outer Glow
    Inner Glow
    Bevel and Emboss
    Colour Fill
    Outline

3. To adjust the properties of a specific effect, select its name and adjust the dialog controls. Adjust the sliders, drop-down menu, or enter specific values to vary each effect. Options differ from one effect to another.

4. Click **OK** to apply the effect or **Cancel** to abandon changes.

Applying 3D layer effects

3D layer effects are just as easy to apply, but they're a bit more complex than their 2D cousins (see p. 83). Actually, there's an easy way to get started with them: simply display the **Instant Effects tab** and preview its gallery thumbnails.

In the tab you'll see a variety of remarkable 3D surface and texture presets grouped into wide-ranging "themed" categories (e.g., Glass Text, Abstract, Wood, Metal). Click any thumbnail to apply it to the active layer. Assuming the layer has some colour on it to start with, you'll see an instant result!

> If hidden, make this tab visible via **Window>Studio Tabs**.

To apply an Instant Effect to the active layer:

- From the **Instant Effects** tab, select a category, then click a gallery thumbnail.

- To make the effect appear smaller or larger in relation to the image, drag the **Scale** slider or type a value in the tab.

You can apply an effect from the Instant Effects tab preset, edit it (using the Layer Effects dialog) and then save it as a custom preset in a user-defined category (you'll have to create and select the category first). To save the preset, right-click in the tab and choose **Add Item...**. From the dialog, you can adjust the Scale of the effect and have your thumbnail preview stored as a Rectangle or as Text (using the letter "A"). For either type, the thumbnail will appear in the gallery.

fx If you want to have complete flexibility when creating 3D effects, you can click the **Add Layer Effects** button on the Layers tab. The dialog is shared for both 2D and 3D effects—simply check the 3D Effects box and experiment with the settings (enable other 3D check boxes as appropriate).

For more information about creating 3D filter effects, see PhotoPlus Help.

3D effects overview

Suppose you've applied a 3D layer effect preset from the Instant Effects tab, and then you bring up the Layer Effects dialog. On inspecting the settings used in the preset, the first thing you'll notice is that several boxes may be checked.

- **3D Effects** is a master switch for this group, and its settings of **Blur** and **Depth** make a great difference; you can click the "+" button to unlink them for independent adjustment.

- **3D Pattern Map** allows for blend mode, opacity, depth, displacement and softening adjustments, along with a choice of gradient fills. This is checked depending on the type of instant effect selected.

- **3D Lighting** provides a "light source" without which any depth information in the effect wouldn't be visible. The lighting settings let you illuminate your 3D landscape and vary its reflective properties.

To apply 3D Effects:

- Click _fx_ **Add Layer Effects** on the Layers tab and check **3D Effects** in the Layer Effects dialog. Adjust the "master control" sliders here to vary the overall properties of any individual 3D effects you select.

  - **Blur** specifies the amount of smoothing applied. Larger blur sizes give the impression of broader, more gradual changes in height.

  - **Depth** specifies how steep the changes in depth appear.

  - The ⊞ button is normally down, which links the two sliders so that sharp changes in Depth are smoothed out by the Blur parameter. To adjust the sliders independently, click the button so it's up (not blue).

- Check a 3D effect in the **3D Effects** list which reflects the 3D effect you can achieve. Procedures for each are detailed below.

3D Reflection Map

The **3D Reflection Map** effect is used to simulate mirrored surfaces by selection of a pattern (i.e., a bitmap which possesses a shiny surface) which "wraps around" a selected object. Patterns which simulate various realistic indoor and outdoor environments can be adopted, with optional use of 3D lighting to further reflect off object edges. The effect is often used in combination with the Transparency option.

Transparency

The uniform transparency of a layer and its objects (with 3D layer effects applied) can be controlled via the Layers tab with the Opacity option (see rear heart shape in example below). However, for more sophisticated transparency control, transparency settings can instead be set within the Layer Effects dialog. The effect can be used to create more realistic transparency by independently controlling transparency on reflective (edges) and non-reflective (flat) areas of the object (see front heart shape below).

Use this effect in conjunction with reflection maps and multiple directional light sources for ultra-realistic glass effects.

*3D Lighting + Layer
Opacity 50%*

*3D Lighting +
Transparency effect*

Warp tool effects

The **Warp Tools** from the [icon] ▾ **Warp Tools flyout** work as a group and act as brush-on effects rather than dialog-based filters. Most of the tools shift pixels as the brush passes over, while the **Unwarp** brush undoes the effects of the other tools. The actual amount of pixel displacement depends on the direction or amount of brush movement, the brush tip, and the tool's settings, selectable from the brush context toolbar.

The [icon] **Elastic Warp Tool** shifts pixels in the direction of brush motion, hence the appearance of pulling or elasticity. Drag across the image to shift pixels in the direction of brush motion. Use for subtle effects such as creating a "smiling" subject.

The [icon] **Pinch** and [icon] **Punch Tools** apply, respectively, a concave or convex spherical distortion under the brush. Wiggle the brush in the region you want to change.

The  **Twirl Tools** produce a "spin art" effect—liquid paint on a surface revolving either clockwise or anti-clockwise around a central point. Wiggle the brush in the region you want to change.

The  **Thick/Thin Warp Tool** shifts pixels 90° to the right of the brush direction, which has the effect of spreading or compressing edges along the stroke. Creatively speaking, if you drag the Thick/Thin tool clockwise, you'll get a concave "pinch" effect, while anti-clockwise motion results in a convex "punch" effect. Drag across the image to shift pixels 90° to the right of the brush direction.

Use the **Unwarp Tool** to reduce the strength of the current warped effect under the brush. Drag the Unwarp brush across a warped region. Note that Unwarp only works as long as you're still using the Warp tools. Similarly, PhotoPlus treats all your operations during one warping session as a single, cumulative event; using the Undo command clears the whole session.

Merging bracketed photos

High Dynamic Range (HDR) merge, or tone mapping, is used to combine bracketed photos or scanned images from film, each shot taken at different exposure levels (typically one each for highlights, midtones, and shadows) and within seconds apart. Your camera can't capture all exposure levels in a single shot, so by bringing together multiple photos you can expand your image's dynamic range which would otherwise be impossible in a single shot.

Typically, scenes of high contrast such as landscapes, sunsets or indoor environments (with strong lighting) are suited to HDR Merge.

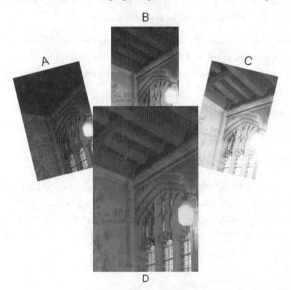

*Exposure for Highlights (**A**), Midtones (**B**), Shadows (**C**),*
*and the Merged output (**D**).*

For good results, it's important to bear the following points in mind:

- Many modern cameras offer **auto-bracketing** which automatically takes several shots at different exposure levels. A two-EV spacing is considered to be optimum for most occasions. Alternatively, shoot with manual exposure set.

- Always shoot the same scene! Your output is based on a composite of the same scene.

- Take as many shots as is needed to cover your required dynamic range.

- Use a tripod for optimum camera stability. Also avoid photographing objects affected by windy conditions (e.g., moving tree branches).

- Ensure **Aperture priority** is set on your camera (see your camera's operating manual for more details).

The HDR merge is a two-stage process, firstly to select the source files (JPG or raw) for merging, and then performing the merge itself after having adjusted merge settings to optimize the output). The process can be carried out directly on source files without loading them into your project in advance.

PhotoPlus lets you optionally save the merged HDR image to one of several formats (namely OpenEXR, HDR and HD Photo), which can be opened at a later date, saving you from having to align and merge your original images again (see p. 93).

To select and merge bracketed photos:

1. From the Startup Wizard, click **HDR Photo Merge.**

2. From the **HDR Source Files** dialog, click **Add**.

3. Browse to, then select multiple files from the chosen folder—use **Ctrl**-click or **Shift**-click for selecting non-adjacent or adjacent images. Click **Open**. The files listed show image name and an exposure value equivalent to your camera's exposure setting (the values are not just for show—they're crucial for successful HDR merging).

Click the **Add** button to add more photos or the **Remove** button to exclude a selected photo.

For scanned images (from camera film) which won't possess EXIF-derived Exposure values, you can click the **Edit Exposure** button to add your own exposure values to entries if you've kept a record (or you could just add +2.0, 0, and -2 then experiment with the results).

4. (Optional) Uncheck **Align images** if you're sure your source images are perfectly aligned (perhaps by a third-party application). Otherwise, PhotoPlus will automatically attempt to align each photo's corresponding pixel data.

5. (Optional) Check **Infer film response curve** to affect a tone curve needed to accurately process scanned images (from camera film). Otherwise, keep unchecked for digital camera use.

6. Click **OK**. The Merge HDR dialog is displayed, showing a preview of your intermediate HDR image.

Don't worry if your initial results look less than desirable. You're only half way towards your stunning image but you'll need to modify the HDR image using a series of adjustments next.

To adjust your intermediate image:

1. From the **HDR Merge** dialog, an image preview is displayed, along with a merge file list and merge settings. Optionally, uncheck an image from the upper-right list to exclude it from the merge.

2. Drag the **Compression** slider to a new value—use your eye to judge the best merge results, but also the supporting Histogram to ensure that the tonal range fits into the visible graph without clipping. The option compresses or expands the dynamic range by dragging right or left, respectively.

3. Set a **Brightness** level to make the image either lighter or darker.

4. Adjust the **Black Point** slider right to shift the histogram's left-most edge making all affected pixels in the shadow region turn black.

5. Reduce **Local Contrast Radius** to alleviate image "flatness" when compressing the dynamic range (see Compression above).

6. Set the **Temperature** to give a warmer "reddish" or cooler "blueish" look; drag to the right or left, respectively.

7. Adjust the **Saturation** value to reduce or boost the colour in your image.

8. Check **Output 16-bits per channel** if you're looking for the highest level of detail in your merged output.

9. Click **OK**.

10. From the next dialog, you'll be asked if you want to save the intermediate HDR Image or just continue as an untitled project.

   • Click **Yes** to preserve the HDR image. This saves having to select, align, and merge images again, but you'll still need to reapply any adjustments previously made. Select a file location, file format, name for your file, then click **Save**. The file format, OpenEXR (.exr), Radiance (.hdr), or HD Photo (.hdp), can be chosen from the drop-down menu.

   OR

   • Click **No** if you don't need to preserve the HDR image (you'll have to select, align, and merge again). Your merge results will be the basis for an Untitled project.

If you've created an intermediate HDR image, it can be opened as for any other file (see p. 20).

5 Manipulating Images

Making a selection

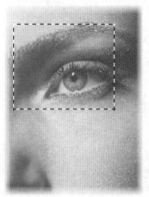

In any photo editing program, the **selection tools and techniques** are as significant as any of the basic brush tools or commands. The basic principle is simple: quite often you'll want to perform an operation on just a portion of the image. To do this you must define an active selection area.

The wide range of selection options in PhotoPlus lets you:

- Define just about any selection shape, using various drawing and painting techniques.

- Modify the extent or properties of the selection (see p. 104)

- Carry out various manipulations on the selected pixels, including cut, copy, paste, rotate, adjust colours, apply special effects, etc. (see p. 108)

Selection basics

Although the techniques for using the various selection methods differ, the end result is always the same: a portion of the active layer has been "roped off" from the rest of the image. The boundary is visible as a broken line or **marquee** around the selected region (see above).

Whenever there's a selection, certain tools and commands operate **only** on the pixels inside the selection—as opposed to a condition where nothing is selected, in which case those functions generally affect the entire active layer.

> You may occasionally (especially if the marquee is hidden) find yourself using a tool or command that seems to have no effect... it's probably because there's still a selection somewhere, and you're trying to work outside the selection. In this case, just cancel the selection.

To cancel the selection (select nothing):

- Right-click and choose **Deselect,** use the **Select** menu or press **Ctrl+D**.

The opposite of selecting nothing is selecting everything:

- To select the entire active layer, press **Ctrl+A**, or choose **Select All** from the **Select** menu.

For partial selection of opaque pixels, you can **Ctrl**-click the layer thumbnail (in Layers tab).

> If your image has multiple layers, and you switch to another layer, the selection doesn't stay on the previous layer—it follows you to the new active layer. This makes sense when you realize that the selection doesn't actually include image content—like an outline map, it just describes a region with boundaries.

Selection tool options

PhotoPlus offers a very wide range of other selection methods, and a variety of commands for modifying the extent or properties of the selected pixels—all available from the Tools toolbar. Note that the selection tools work on Background and standard layers, but not on text layers or shape layers.

Available from:	Tools
Selection Tools flyout	**Rectangle Selection Tool**—drag out a rectangular selection area of your chosen size (use the **Ctrl** key to constrain to a Square area).
	Ellipse Selection Tool—drag out an ellipse selection area (use **Ctrl** key to constrain to a circle).
	QuickShape Selection Tools flyout—provides different variable shapes, including pie, star, arrow, heart, spiral, wave, and so on. The shapes can be further "morphed" into other custom QuickShapes by dragging node handles around the QuickShape.

Lasso Tools
flyout

Freehand Selection Tool—lets you draw a freehand (irregular) line which is closed automatically to create an irregularly shaped selection area.

Polygon Selection Tool—lets you draw a series of straight-line segments (double-click to close the polygon).

Magnetic Selection Tool—lets you trace around an object edge creating a selection line that snaps to the edge as you drag.

directly from
toolbar

Magic Wand Tool—lets you select a region based on the colour similarity of adjacent pixels—simply click a starting pixel then set a **Tolerance** from the context toolbar. It works much like the fill tool, but the result is a selected region rather than a region flooded with a colour.

directly from
toolbar

Selection Brush Tool—lets you paint your selection as a series of brush strokes.

T ▾
Text Tools
flyout

Text Selection Tool—lets you create a selection in the form of text. Click with the tool to display the Text cursor. Type your text, format as needed, and click **OK**. (See Creating and Editing text.)

For any selection tool, the Context toolbar includes combination buttons (**New**, **Add**, **Subtract**, and **Intersect**) that determine the effect of each new selection operation.

For example, starting with a square selection (created with the **New** button), here's what a second partly overlaid square (shown with a solid line) might produce with each setting:

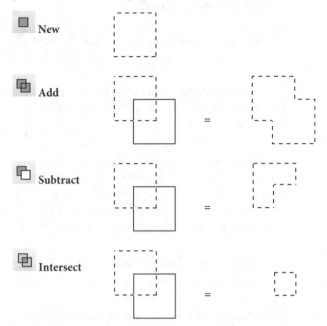

For Rectangle and Ellipse Selection tools, the Context toolbar additionally lets you set a **Fixed Size** or **Fixed Aspect**, or number of Rows or Columns (Rectangle Selection Tool only) in advance of creating your selection—great if you have a clear idea of the selection area required!

Using the Selection Brush Tool is a simple way to create a brush-based selection. For a more sophisticated selection method, utilizing full brush control and painting in greyscale for degrees of selectiveness, use **Paint to Select** mode. (See Paint to Select mode on p. 107.)

Selecting layer opacity/transparency

New layers are transparent (they have an alpha channel), but once you've placed pixels on the layer you'll be able to select between the layer's pixels (i.e., their opacity) and remaining transparency.

To create a selection from a layer's opacity/transparency:

- For selection of **Opacity**: In the Layers tab, **Ctrl**-click on the layer's image thumbnail.

- For selection of **Transparency**: As above, but additionally select **Invert** from the **Select** menu.

Colour Range

As an intelligent colour selection method, i.e. where selection is based on "tagging" a specific range of colours or tones in the image, choose **Colour Range** from the **Select** menu.

To select a colour range:

1. Choose **Colour Range...** from the **Select** menu. The Colour Range dialog appears, with the image visible in the main Preview window.

2. To make an initial selection:

   - To tag a particular colour or tone group, such as "Reds" or "Midtones," choose the group's name from the **Select** drop-down list.
     OR

     Click ![picker] **Colour Picker** to sample a chosen pixel colour under the visible dropper cursor. With this method, the **Tolerance** slider lets you include a wider or narrower range of colours in the selection, based on the chosen colour.

![tools] Once you've made an initial selection, you can use the **Add Colour** and **Subtract Colour** buttons to include/exclude further colours in the selection by single-click or by dragging across the image to tag/untag a colour range. Alternatively, for initial selection, drag across the image to select ranges.

> With **Add/Subtract Colour** tools initially selected, you can also drag across a section of the image.

Meanwhile, the dialog provides visual feedback.

1. If **Show Selection** is checked, the greyscale Selection window on the right shows tagged values as brighter, with untagged pixels darker. To customize what's displayed in the Preview window on the left, choose an option from the Preview list: "None" shows the original image, "White Matte" shows tagged pixels through a white background, and so on.

2. Click **OK** to confirm the selection, or **Cancel** to abandon changes. **Reset** reverts back to original dialog settings.

Storing selections

You can **store selections** (i.e., just the marqueed region and per-pixel selectedness data) as part of either the current image or any open image file, and **load** a stored selection at any time. It's often useful to be able to "grab" the same region of an image at different phases of working on it. And, for repetitive tasks (preparing web buttons, for example) on different but graphically similar files, by storing a selection you can reuse it rather than having to recreate it for each file.

Selections are created and stored exclusively as alpha channels in the Channels tab; Once stored, they can be retrieved from the tab at any time.

As each alpha channel behaves like a mask (p. 45) you can paint on the alpha channel at different greyscale levels for different levels of "selectedness". The White or light portions of the mask reveal layer pixels (make them more opaque). Black or dark portions hide layer pixels (making them more transparent).

To store a selection:

1. Make a selection on your image.

2. In the Channels tab, select ▢ **Create Channel From Selection**. The channel appears with a default name (rename via double-click if needed).

> 💡 Use ⊞ **New Channel** on the Channels tab to create an empty channel on which you can design (e.g., paint) in greyscale for different levels of "selectedness".

To load a selection:

- In the Channels tab, select ▢ **Create Selection From Channel**.

To delete a stored selection:

- In the Channels tab, select 🗑 **Delete Channel**.

Modifying a selection

Once you've used a selection tool to select a region on the active layer, you can carry out a number of additional steps to fine-tune the selection before you actually apply an effect or manipulation to the selected pixels. Paint to Select mode even lets you use standard painting or editing tools as selection tools!

Transforming the selection

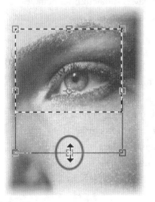

The **Selection Deform Tool** on the **Tools** toolbar's **Deform Tools** flyout lets you transform, scale or rotate any already drawn selection area. With the tool enabled, square nodes on the mid-points and corners of any selected area can be dragged (opposite).

Look for the cursor changing between resize and rotate modes when hovering over a corner node.

Use in conjunction with the **Ctrl** key to transform the selection area without constraint, creating a **skewed transform** (drag nodes as appropriate). The **Alt** key resizes the area about its centre, while the **Shift** key maintains the area's aspect ratio. It's also possible to move the small centre of rotation "handle" in the centre of the transform to produce an arc rotational movement rather than rotating around the area's centre (by default).

> Holding down the **Shift** key whilst rotating will cause a movement in 15 degree intervals.

Making the selection larger or smaller

If the selection you've made isn't quite the right shape, or doesn't quite include all the necessary pixels (or perhaps includes a few too many), you can continue to use the selection tools to add to, or subtract from, the selected region.

To add or subtract to/from the existing selection with a selection tool:

- Select the tool and drag while holding down the **Shift** or **Alt** key, respectively. The newly selected pixels don't have to adjoin the current selection—it's possible to select two or more separate regions on the active layer.

Modifying the selection

Once you've made a selection, several modify selection operations can be used in combination to alter the selection area. Feather, smooth, contract, and expand operations are possible from a single **Modify Selection** dialog, along with the popular Grow, Similar, and Invert available separately. Combining the operations in a dialog improves efficiency, and lets you preview your modified selection **directly on the page** as you make changes. Several preview methods are possible.

To modify a current selection:

1. From any Selection context toolbar, select **Modify Selection...**.

2. From the **Modify Selection** dialog, you can enter a specific pixel value for the type of operation you require.

   - **Feather**: Use to apply feathering "after the fact" to an existing selection (but before applying any editing changes). Enter the width (in pixels) of the transition area. A higher value produces a wider, more gradual fade-out. See Soft-edged and hard-edged selections below.

- **Smooth**: If the selected region has ragged edges or discontinuous regions (for example, if you've just used the Magic Wand Tool), use the option to control the extent of smoothing.

- **Contract/Expand**: Move the slider left to contract (shrink) the borders of the selection, or right to extend its borders.

3. Select a preview method from the **Preview** drop-down list—choose to preview as an Overlay, in Greyscale, or use different Mattes.

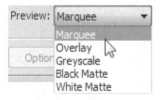

The **Modify** item on the **Select** menu (or right-click on selection) provides a submenu with the above options, along with other intelligent selection options:

- **Grow** and **Similar** both expand the selection by seeking out pixels close (in colour terms) to those in the current selection. **Grow** only adds pixels adjacent to the current selection, while **Similar** extends the selection to any similar pixels in the active layer.
  Both options use the tolerance setting entered for the Magic Wand Tool on the Context toolbar. As the tolerance increases, a larger region is selected. Typically when using these tools, you'll start by selecting a very small region (the particular colour you want to "find" in the rest of the image).

- Choose **Border...** to create a new selection as a "frame" of a specified pixel width around the current selection.

- The **Invert** option selects the portion of the active layer outside the current selection. Unselected pixels become selected, and vice versa.

Soft-edged and hard-edged selections

Anti-aliasing and **feathering** are different ways of controlling what happens at the edges of a selection. Both produce softer edges that result in smoother blending of elements that are being combined in the image. You can control either option for the Standard and QuickShape Selection tools, using the **Feather** input box (or slider) and **Anti-alias** check box on the Context toolbar.

- **Anti-aliasing** produces visibly smooth edges by making the selection's edge pixels semi-transparent. (As a layer option, it's not available on the Background layer, which doesn't support transparency.)

- If an anti-aliased selection (for example, one pasted from another image) includes partially opaque white or black edge pixels, you can use **Matting** options on the **Layers** menu to remove these pixels from the edge region, yielding a smoother blend between the selection and the image content below. (Fully opaque edge pixels are not affected.)

- **Feathering** reduces the sharpness of a selection's edges, not by varying transparency, but by *partially selecting* edge pixels. If you lay down paint on a feathered selection, the paint will actually be less intense around the edges.

- **Threshold** converts a feathered, soft-edged selection into a hard-edged selection (use **Modify>Threshold**). As with feathering, you won't see an immediate effect on the image, but painting and other editing operations will work differently inside the selection.

Paint to Select mode

The Brush Selection Tool lets you paint a selection. However, as a more advanced feature, **Paint to Select** mode lets you:

- use finer brush control to modify your selection.

- modify the selection using standard painting and editing tools according to the lightness of the colours you apply.

See PhotoPlus Help for more information.

Manipulating a selection

Moving the selection marquee

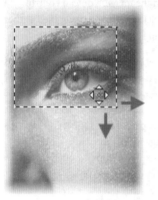

Sometimes, you need to adjust the position of the marquee without affecting the underlying pixels. Any time you're using one of the selection tools, the cursor over a selected region changes to the **Move Marquee** cursor, which lets you drag the marquee outline to reposition it.

> 🔖 You're only moving the selection outline—not the image content inside it.
>
> 💡 You can also use the keyboard arrows to "nudge" the selection marquee.

Once you have selected your chosen pixels, the operations which can be performed include moving, cutting, copying, duplicating, pasting and deleting. You use the **Move Tool** to drag the selection *plus* its image content. (See Modifying a selection on p. 104).

Using the Move Tool

The **Move Tool** is for pushing actual pixels around. With it, you can drag the content of a selection from one place to another, rather than just moving the selection outline. To use it, simply click on the selection and drag to the new location. The selected part of the image moves also.

- If nothing is selected, dragging with the Move Tool moves the entire active layer. (Or, if the Move Tool's **Automatically select layer** property is selected on its context toolbar, the tool moves the first visible item's layer beneath the move cursor when you click to move.)

- When the Move Tool is chosen, you can also use the keyboard arrows to "nudge" the selection or active layer.

- The "hole" left behind when the image content is moved exposes the current background colour (on the Background layer), or transparency (see above; on standard layers), shown with a "checkerboard" pattern.

- To duplicate the contents of the selection on the active layer, press the **Alt** key and click, then drag with the Move Tool.

- As a shortcut if you're working with any one of the selection tools, you can press the **Ctrl** key to switch temporarily to the Move Tool. Press **Ctrl+Alt** to duplicate. Release the key(s) to revert to the selection tool.

Cut/Copy/Delete/Paste

Cut and copy operations on selections involving the Clipboard work just as in other Windows programs.

- To copy pixels in the selected region, press **Ctrl-C** or click the ⬚ **Copy** button on the **Standard** toolbar. (You can also choose **Copy** from the **Edit** menu.)

- To cut the selected pixels, press **Ctrl-X** or choose **Cut** from the **Edit** menu.

- To delete the selected pixels, press the **Delete** key or choose **Clear** from the **Edit** menu.

Cut or deleted pixels expose the current background colour (on the Background layer) or transparency (on standard layers). If you want to create transparency on the Background layer, first "promote" it to a standard layer by right-clicking its name on the Layers tab and choosing **Promote to Layer**.

- If nothing is selected, a cut or copy operation affects the whole active layer, as if **Select All** were in effect.

When pasting from the Clipboard, PhotoPlus offers several options.

- To paste as a new image in an untitled window, press **Ctrl+V** or click the **Paste as New image** button on the **Standard** toolbar. (Or select from the **Edit>Paste** menu.)

- To paste as a new layer above the active layer, press **Ctrl+L** or choose **Paste>As New Layer** from the **Edit** menu.

- To paste into the current selection, press **Shift+Ctrl+L** or choose **Paste> Into Selection** from the **Edit** menu. The Clipboard contents appear centred in the currently selected region. (This choice is greyed out if there's no selection, or if the active layer is a text layer.) This option is useful if you're pasting from one layer to another. Because the selection marquee "follows" you to the new layer, you can use it to keep the pasted contents in registration with the previous layer.

- To duplicate part of the active layer on the same layer, press the **Alt** key and click, then drag with the Move Tool. (Or if you're working with a selection tool, press **Ctrl+Alt** and drag to duplicate.)

Changing image and canvas size

You probably know that image dimensions are given in **pixels** (think of pixels as the "dots of paint" that comprise a screen image)—say, 1024 wide by 768 high. If you want to change these dimensions, there are two ways to go about it, and that's where **image** and **canvas** come into play.

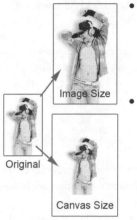

- Changing the **image size** (top example opposite) means scaling the whole image (or just a selected region) up or down. Resizing is actually a kind of distortion because the image content is being stretched or squashed.

- Changing the **canvas size** (bottom example) just involves adding or taking away pixels around the edges of the image. It's like adding to the neutral border around a mounted photo, or taking a pair of scissors and cropping the photo to a smaller size. In either case, the remaining image pixels are undisturbed so there's no distortion.

Note that once you've changed either the image size or the canvas size, the image and canvas are exactly the same size again!

Changing image size

The **Image Size** dialog lets you specify a new size for the whole image, in terms of its screen dimensions and/or printed dimensions.

To resize the whole image:

1. Choose **Image Size...** from the **Image** menu.

2. To specify just the printed dimensions, uncheck **Resize layers**. Check the box to link the Pixel Size (screen) settings to the Print Size or Resolution settings.

3. To retain the current image proportions, check **Maintain aspect ratio**. Uncheck the box to alter the dimensions independently.

4. If adjusting screen dimensions:

   • Select a preferred scale (either "Pixels" or "Percent") in the drop-down list.

   • Select a resampling method. As a rule, use Nearest Pixel for hard-edge images, Bilinear Interpolation when shrinking photos, Bicubic Interpolation when enlarging photos, and Lanczos3 Window when best quality results are expected.

5. If adjusting printed dimensions, select your preferred units of measurement and resolution. The pixel size will automatically alter with print size adjustment.

6. Enter the new values and click **OK**.

Changing canvas size

There are several ways of changing the canvas size that was originally chosen when creating a new image (see p. 18). If you just want to reduce the canvas area, you can use the **Crop Tool** (see Cropping an image on p. 113) or the **Image>Crop to Selection** command. To either enlarge or reduce the canvas, the **Image>Canvas Size...** command provides a dialog that lets you specify where pixels should be added or subtracted.

To change canvas size:

1. Choose **Canvas Size...** from the **Image** menu.

2. Enter **New Width** and/or **New Height** values (the current values are also shown for comparison). Alternatively, select the **Relative** check box to enter the number of units you want to add or subtract from the existing width and height values—for example, 5 pixels, 1 cm, 100 points, 10 percent, and so on.

3. In the Anchor box, click to position the image thumbnail with respect to edges where pixels should be added or subtracted. For example, if you want to extend the canvas from all sides of the image, click the centre anchor point.

4. Click **OK**.

> If the canvas size is increased, the new canvas area is filled (on the Background layer) with the current background colour and (on standard layers) with transparency.

Cropping an image

Cropping is the electronic equivalent of taking a pair of scissors to a photograph, except of course with a pair of scissors there is no second chance! Cropping deletes all of the pixels outside the crop selection area, and then resizes the image canvas so that only the area inside the crop selection remains. Use it to focus on an area of interest—either for practical reasons or to improve photo composition.

Before

After
(Rectangular Crop)

PhotoPlus allows you to crop unconstrained, or to a standard or custom print size.

To crop unconstrained:

1. From the Tools toolbar's ⬜ ▾ **Crop Tools** flyout, select the ⬜ **Crop Tool**. Ensure the **Unconstrained** option is set in the Context toolbar's first drop-down list.

2. Drag out a rectangle to create an unconstrained rectangle, then fine-tune the areas dimensions if needed by dragging the edges. Note that you can also constrain the crop area to be a square, by holding down the **Ctrl** key while dragging.

3. To crop to the designated size, double-click inside the crop area.

The **Shading** check box and **Opacity** option on the Context toolbar sets the shade colour and transparency of the unwanted region outside the rectangle, respectively. Uncheck Shading to view only the rectangle, with no shading and full transparency.

> Cropping with the Crop Tool affects all image layers. Everything outside the designated region is eliminated. If there's a marquee-based selection, it is ignored and deselected during cropping.

To crop to a specific print size or resolution:

1. Select the ⬜ **Crop Tool** from the Tools toolbar.

2. Then either:

   - For print sizes, choose a **pre-defined** print size (expressed in inches) from the first drop-down menu in the Context toolbar. Both portrait and landscape crop regions can be selected—e.g., 4 x 6 in for portrait, 6 x 4 in for landscape).

   OR

   - If you need to set a **custom** size, enter values into the Height and Width drop-down menus, choosing inches or centimetres as measurement units in advance—note that the print size changes to "Custom" after entering new values. The Print Size resolution alters automatically while honouring your print Width and Height.

3. Drag out your crop area to create your constrained rectangle or square (if Custom).

4. Double-click the crop area to crop to the designated size.

Use the **Thirds grid** check box on the Context toolbar for improving photo composition. A 3 x 3 rectangular grid with equally spaced lines (two vertically, two horizontally) is superimposed on top of your photo when the check box is selected.

Moving and resizing the grid allows the main subject of your photo (in this case a big wheel) to be offset and balanced against a foreground or background feature within the photo (e.g., the sky as background). Position a main item of interest in the photo where any two lines intersect within the crop grid (four intersections are possible). This is known as the "rule of thirds" which will help you find the most balanced composition where your eyes are drawn to the main subject. Double-click to crop the photo to the outer grid dimensions.

You can also crop an image to any **selection area**, no matter what shape, as defined with one of the selection tools. For example, here's cropping applied to a selection created with a QuickShape Selection Tool, called the Thought Selection Tool.

To crop the image to the selection:

- Choose **Crop to Selection** from the **Image** menu.

If the selection region is non-rectangular, the left-over surrounding region will be either transparent (on a standard layer) or the current background colour (e.g., white).

> Cropping to the selection affects all image layers. Everything outside the selected region is eliminated.

Flipping and rotating

Flipping and rotating are standard manipulations that you can carry out on the whole image, the active layer, a path, or just on a selection. Flips are used to change the direction of a subject's gaze, fix composition, and so on, whereas rotation is an orientation tool for general purpose use.

Flip Horizontal

Flip Vertical

Rotate – 15° anti-clockwise

Rotate – 10° clockwise

To flip:

- Choose either **Flip Horizontally** or **Flip Vertically** from the **Image** menu, then select **Image**, **Layer**, **Selection** or **Path** from the submenu.

To rotate:

1. Choose **Rotate** from the **Image** menu.

2. From the flyout menu, select an option based on the object (Image, Layer, or Selection), rotation angle (90° or 180°), and the direction (Clockwise or Anticlockwise) required.

3. You can also select **Custom...**, to display a Rotate dialog, from which you can do all of the above but instead set your own custom angle, even down to fractional degrees.

Deforming

The **Deform Tool** lets you move, scale, rotate, or skew a selection or layer. Start by making a selection if desired, then choose the Deform Tool. For either selection or layer, a rectangle appears with handles at its corners and edges, and a fixed point (initially in the centre of the region). If there's no selection, the rectangle includes the whole active layer.

For example, a layer can be deformed using scale and skew operations.

Scale *down layer contents from top-right corner of rectangle; revealing the background colour.*

Skew *from top-right corner handle by dragging with the* **Ctrl** *key pressed.*

The layer contents are skewed for artistic effect.

The tool's action depends on the exact position of the mouse pointer. As you move the pointer around the enclosed region, the cursor changes as shown below to indicate which action is possible.

▶ To **move the region** without any deformation, drag from its neutral midsection. This action works just like the Move Tool.

To **reshape the region**, drag from an edge or corner handle. A variety of options are available (watch the Hintline for tips).

 • **Over a corner handle:**

  • Drag to scale region in two dimensions (height and width).

  • To maintain constant proportions, drag with the **Shift** key down.

  • To scale the region relative to the fixed point, drag with the **Alt** key down. Pixels further from the fixed point will move further than those close to it.

  • To freely distort the region from one corner, drag with the **Ctrl** key down.

  • To scale relative to the fixed point with constant proportions, drag while pressing **Shift+Alt**.

  • To distort relative to the fixed point, drag while pressing **Ctrl+Alt**. The opposite corner mirrors the dragged corner's movement.

  • To distort the region along either adjacent edge, drag while pressing **Shift+Ctrl**.

  • For a perspective effect, drag while pressing **Shift+Ctrl+Alt**. The adjacent corner mirrors the dragged corner's movement.

- **Over an edge handle:**

  - Drag to move the edge in or out, for a squash/stretch effect.

  - For a squash/stretch effect relative to the fixed point, drag with the **Alt** key down. Pixels further from the fixed point will move further than those close to it.

  - To move the edge freely, for a skew effect, drag with the **Ctrl** key down.

  - For a skew effect relative to the fixed point, drag while pressing **Ctrl+Alt**. The opposite edge mirrors the dragged edge's movement.

  - For a constrained skew effect, press **Shift+Ctrl** and drag the edge along its line.

  - For constrained skew relative to the fixed point, press **Shift+Ctrl+Alt** and drag the edge along its line.

To **rotate the region** about the fixed point, drag from just outside a corner. To constrain rotation in 15-degree steps, press the **Shift** key after you've begun rotation, and hold it down until after you release the mouse button. You can change the location of the fixed point (see below).

To **reposition the fixed point**, move the cursor to the exact centre until a small target appears, then drag. The fixed point can be moved anywhere—even outside the deformation region. Great for arced rotations.

For even more sophisticated warping effects, you can use mesh warping (see p. 120). Aside from minor cursor differences, the above instructions also apply to the **Deform Mesh Tool** included on the Mesh Warp Tool's Context toolbar.

Mesh warping

The  **Mesh Warp Tool** works like the Deform Tool outfitted with complex curves. It lets you define a flexible grid of points and lines that you can drag to distort an image, or part of an image (or layer). You can edit the mesh to vary its curvature, and even custom-design a mesh to match a particular image's geometry—for example, curves that follow facial contours—for more precise control of the warp effect.

> The Mesh Warp Tool works on Background and standard layers, but not on text layers or shape layers.

When you first select the tool, a simple rectangular mesh appears over the image, with nine nodes: one at each corner, one at the centre, and one at the midpoint of each edge. Straight lines connect adjacent nodes. A context toolbar also appears to support the Mesh Warp Tool.

The straight line segments are actually bendable curves. When you alter the contours of the mesh and distort the initial rectangular grid, the underlying image deforms accordingly. To change the mesh, you simply move nodes, node attractor handles, or connecting lines; add or subtract nodes as needed; and/or edit nodes to change the curvature of adjoining lines.

To select a mesh node:

- Click it. (**Shift**-click or drag a marquee to select multiple nodes.)

One or more attractor handles appear on the selected node(s) and on any adjacent nodes. The number of handles per node will vary depending on the number of adjacent nodes.

To warp the mesh:

- Drag a mesh node to move it.
  OR

- Drag a line segment to reshape it.
  OR

- Drag a node's attractor handles.

To add a new node:

- Double-click on a line segment.
  OR

- Click on a line segment then select the ⌖ **Add Node** button on the displayed Context toolbar.

The new node appears, along with extra nodes where the new connecting lines intersect existing lines. Adding a new node further subdivides the mesh.

To delete one or more nodes:

1. Select the node(s).

2. Press **Delete**.
   OR

   Click the ⌖ **Delete node(s)** button on the displayed Context toolbar.

Deleting a node also deletes lines and nodes connected to it. If you delete a corner or edge node, the overall mesh area will decrease. To delete a specific grid line and its nodes, click to place a marker on the line, then press **Delete**.

The bendability of line segments depends on the type of nodes at either end. You can change a node from one type to another simply by selecting it and using the Context toolbar buttons:

Mesh nodes can be **sharp**, **smooth**, or **symmetric** (see illustrations below). Changing a node's type lets you control how much the curved segments bend on either side of the node. To determine a node's current type, select it and check to see which Mesh Node button on the toolbar is also selected.

To change a node to a different type:

- Select it and click one of the other node buttons.

Experiment, and you'll begin to appreciate the fine control that these settings afford. For example, using a light-blue Quick Grill shape, it's easy to appreciate the difference between node types.

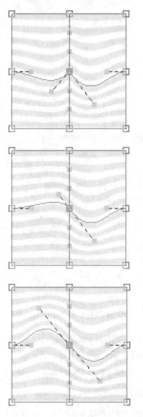

Sharp means that the slope and depth of the curves on either side of the node are completely independent of each other. The contours can be adjusted separately, and the intersection can be pointed.

Smooth means that the slope of the curve is the same on both sides of the node, but the depth of the contours on either side can differ.

Symmetric nodes join curves with the same slope and depth on both sides of the node.

To reset the mesh to full-frame and rectangular:

- Click the ⊞ **Reset Mesh** button on the Mesh Context toolbar.

To hide the mesh for a better preview of the image:

- Click the ⊞ **Hide/Show Mesh** button on the Mesh Context toolbar. Click again to reveal the mesh for editing.

The **Deform Mesh** option makes it easy to move, scale, skew, or rotate a mesh **region** about a fixed point; a region is the area enclosed by multiple nodes. It works just like the standard Deform tool (described above) but on multiple nodes instead of individual ones.

To deform the mesh systematically:

1. **Shift**-click or drag a marquee to select multiple nodes.

2. Click the 🔖 **Deform Mesh** button on the Mesh Warp Tool's Context toolbar. A red selection rectangle appears around the designated nodes (you may need to zoom in to see this), with a fixed point in the centre and handles at its corners, sides, and centre.

   - To deform the mesh region, drag from any corner or midpoint handle.

   - To rotate the mesh region, drag from just outside any corner handle.

   - To move the fixed point, move the cursor over the fixed point symbol until the cursor changes, then drag (this then lets you perform arc rotations). To move the entire region, drag from elsewhere within the region.

   - Watch the Hintline for details on many key-assisted options such as skew, squash/stretch, and perspective effects. In this respect, the tool works almost exactly like the regular Deform Tool (see p. 117).

3. Click the button again to return to standard mesh warping.

Using Image Cutout Studio

Image Cutout Studio offers a powerful integrated solution for cutting out part of an image on an active Background or standard layer. In doing so, you can separate subject of interests from their backgrounds, either by retaining the subject of interest (usually people, objects, etc.) or removing a simple uniform background (e.g., sky, studio backdrop). In both instances, the resulting "cutout" creates an eye-catching look for your image, and lets you present cutouts layer-by-layer—great for simulating subject/background combinations and artistic collages.

The latter background removal method is illustrated in the following multi-image example.

The white initial background is discarded, leaving interim checkerboard transparency, from which another image can be used as a more attractive background. A red tint on the second image's background is used to indicate areas to be discarded.

> Image Cutout Studio works on Background and standard layers, but not on text layers or shape layers.

To launch Image Cutout Studio:

1. Select an image to be cut out.

2. Select **Cutout Studio** from the Photo Studio toolbar.

    OR

    Select **Cutout Studio...** from the **Edit** menu.

Image Cutout Studio is launched.

Changing output settings

You can set the level of transparency and pixel blending at the cutout edge by adjusting the output settings, **Width** and **Blur**. Control of the cutout edge lets you blend your cutout into new backgrounds more realistically.

To change output settings:

1. Drag the **Width** slider to set the extent (in pixels) to which "alpha" blending is applied inside the cutout edge. This creates an offset region within which blending occurs.

2. Adjust the **Blur** slider to apply a level of smoothing to the region created by the above Width setting.

> You'll need to click ⊚ **Preview** in order to check output setting adjustments each time.

Selecting areas to keep or discard

A pair of brushes for keeping and discarding is used to "paint" areas on your active layer. The tools are called **Keep Brush** and **Discard Brush**, and are either used independently or, more typically, in combination with each other. When using either tool, the brush paints an area contained by an outline which is considered to be retained or discarded (depending on brush type). A configurable number of pixels adjacent to the outline area are blended.

 To aid the selection operation, several display modes are available to show selection.

 Show Original, **Show Tinted**, and **Show Transparent** buttons respectively display the image with:

*   selection areas only

*   various coloured tints aiding complex selection operations

*   checkerboard transparency areas marked for discarding.

For Show Tinted, a red tint indicates areas to be discarded; a green tint shows areas to be kept.

For Show transparent mode, a different **Background colour** can be set (at bottom of the Studio) which might help differentiate areas to keep or discard.

To select areas for keeping/discarding:

1. In Image Cutout Studio, click either **Keep Brush Tool** or **Discard Brush Tool** from the left of the Studio workspace.

2. (Optional) Pick a **Brush size** suitable for the area to be worked on.

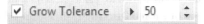

3. (Optional) Set a **Grow tolerance** value to automatically expand the selected area under the cursor (by detecting colours similar to those within the current selection). The greater the value the more the selected area will grow.

> ✔ Grow Tolerance   ▸ 50   ⬍

4. Using the circular cursor, click and drag across the area to be retained or discarded (depending on Keep or Discard Brush Tool selection). It's OK to repeatedly click and drag until your selection area is made.

The **Undo** button reverts to the last made selection.

💡 To fine-tune your selection, you can switch between Keep and Discard brushes by temporarily holding down the **Alt** key.

5. Click **OK** to create your cutout.

You'll now see your active layer with the selected areas cut away (made transparent).

💡 Click **Reset** if you want to revert your selected areas and start your cutout again.

Refining your cutout area

Erase and Restore touch-up tools can be used to refine the cutout area within the studio before completing your cutout.

> The touch-up tools are brush based and are only to be used to fine-tune your almost complete cutout—use your Keep and Discard brush tools for the bulk of your work!

To restore or remove portions of your cutout:

1. With your cutout areas already defined, click ⦾ **Preview** (Output settings tab). You can use the button to check your cutout as you progress.

2. Click the **Restore Touch-up Tool** or **Erase Touch-up Tool** button from the left of the Studio workspace.

3. Paint the areas for restoring or erasing as you would with the brush tools.

> If you've touched up part of your image between each preview, you'll be asked if you want to save or discard changes.

Using channels

Every colour photo that you use in PhotoPlus will have channels associated with it. For the colour mode RGB, the individual channels Red (R), Green (G) and Blue (B) make up a composite RGB channel. Alternatively, channels can also be separate, i.e. as their individual colours—Red, Green and Blue. Each channel stores that particular colour's information which, when combined with the other channels, brings about the full colour image.

> Within PhotoPlus, channels are treated as a colour sub-set of the active selected layer, whether this is a background, standard, shape or text layer.

PhotoPlus lets you show, hide, and select composite or specific channels of any photo from a single point, called the Channels tab. This tab lists the composite RGB and each individual Red, Green and Blue channel in turn.

> If hidden, make this tab visible via **Window>Studio Tabs**.

By default, all channels are selected and visible (see opposite).

If hidden, make this tab visible via **Window>Studio Tabs**.

Why do we want to select channels anyway? This is because you can apply an edit to an individual channel in isolation. Typically, you could:

- Apply a filter effect

- Make an image adjustment

- Paint onto a channel

- Paste selections

- Apply a colour fill

- Apply a mask

To hide/show channels:

1. Select the **Channels** tab.

2. Click the eye button next to the channel(s) (it doesn't have to be selected) to make it hidden. When the button is clicked again, the channel is made visible.

The composite RGB channel is shown only when all the other channels are shown. When only a single or pair of single channels is shown the composite channel will never be shown.

To select specific channels for edit:

1. Select the **Channels** tab. All channels are switched on and are shown by default.

2. Click on the channel you want to select—the other channels will be deselected and hidden automatically. Use **Shift**-click to include additional channels if necessary.

3. Apply the adjustment, special effect, painting operation, etc. to the selected channel(s).

Alpha channel editing

The Channels tab lets you create 8-bit alpha channels, used for masking and storing selections. Typically, you would use each alpha channel as a channel mask, which means you can draw paint in greyscale or fill selections on the created alpha channel. As you paint you can alter the **Greyscale** level in the Colour tab to control the transparency/opacity level. See Using masks on p. 45 for more information.

To create an alpha channel:

1. On the **Channels** tab, click ⊞ **New Channel**. Only the alpha channel is selected and displayed.

2. Paint or create selections on the selected alpha channel to mask out areas of your image. Drawn regions can be painted in white (to remove areas) or black (to retain areas).

PhotoPlus also lets you store selections as separate alpha channels. Selections are made by using the Magic Wand Tool, Selection Brush Tool, and various shape selection tools. At any point, you can reinstate your stored selection, aiding productivity. See Storing selections on p. 102 for more details.

Interpreting histograms

The Histogram tab is used to view the distribution of colours and tones spread throughout your current selection, selected layer or entire photo (by default). This gives an opportunity to view and interpret a complete snapshot of the range of colours and, most importantly, the distribution of pixels that adopt those colours.

The histogram doesn't carry out any adjustments by itself, but it is useful for evaluating the kinds of image adjustments that may be needed. This decision is up to the user and his/her own personal judgement.

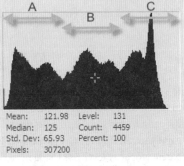

pixel count

Mean:	121.98	Level:	131
Median:	125	Count:	4459
Std. Dev:	65.93	Percent:	100
Pixels:	307200		

0<------------tonal range--------->255

For example, we'll use the composite RGB channel for clarity (although you'll get all colours by default). Think of the histogram as being split into three portions—(**A**) **Shadows**, (**B**) **Midtones**, and (**C**) **Highlights**.

For any channel, the horizontal X axis represents the range of tones, each tone is at a specific level.

The vertical Y axis is the relative **pixel count** at each of the levels on the X axis described above. The higher the graph is at any level, the more pixels reside at that particular level. Remember that this histogram could refer to a Red, Green, Blue, RGB or luminance channel.

A crosshair cursor can be moved around the histogram, displaying the pixel count for the colour level that your cursor is currently placed at. For example, the tab above shows the cursor at colour level 131, which has a count of 4459 pixels.

You can choose to view the histogram for an individual Red, Green or Blue channel, All colours, or the composite of the three, the RGB channel. Luminance (or lightness) can also be shown. See PhotoPlus Help for more information.

6 Painting & Drawing

Colour concepts

Colour modes

PhotoPlus operates in several colour modes to let you work in standard and higher levels of colour or tonal detail—these are 8-bits/channel RGB (or 8-bits/channel Greyscale) and the more detailed 16-bits/channel RGB (or 16-bits/channel Greyscale). Editing in 8 bits/channel mode will use 256 levels per colour channel, as opposed to 16-bits/channel, which uses 65,536 levels per channel.

As a rule of thumb, use 16-bit working for "as-your-eyes-see-it" image accuracy.

If you work with 16-bit images, you'll probably want to benefit from the optimum colour or tonal information throughout your project. In fact, 16-bits/channel colour mode is invoked **automatically** when:

- importing a raw image from Raw Studio.

- opening a 16-bit Microsoft HD photo.

PhotoPlus also lets you **manually** choose modes:

	Choose..	Then pick...
when creating a new image	**New Image** (Startup Wizard) or **File>New**	Colour Mode: RGB or Greyscale Bit Depth: 8 or 16 bits per channel
at any time	**Image>Colour Mode**	RGB 8 Bits/Channel RGB 16 Bits/Channel Greyscale 8 Bits/Channel Greyscale 16 Bits/Channel
when outputting the results of an HDR Merge	**File>HDR Merge...**	Output 16-bits per channel

At some point, you may have no need to work at a high level of detail (16 Bits/channel). In converting to 8-bit mode, you may want to opt for smaller file sizes or take advantage of PhotoPlus's range of special filter effects.

To switch from 16-bits/channel to 8-bits/channel working:

- From the **Image** menu, select **Colour Mode**, and pick an 8-bits/channel option from the submenu.

Like most 16-bit photo editing programs, the choice of filter effects available is limited while in a 16-bits/channel mode.

There's no real benefit in converting 8 bit images to 16 bit as you don't gain any additional image data.

To check which mode is currently set, the Title bar shows the mode after the file name, e.g. CRW_4832.CRW @ 20%, 3088 x 2056, **RGB 16 Bits/Channel**.

Choosing colours

Foreground and background colours

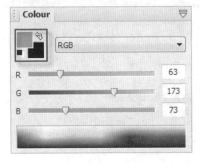

At any given time, PhotoPlus allows you to work with just two colours—a **foreground** colour and a **background** colour. These are always visible as two swatches on the Colour tab indicated opposite.

The foreground colour is set to green (RGB 63:173:73) and the background colour to black.

The Colour tab makes it possible to set the working colour model before colour selection: **RGB** (Red, Green, Blue); **CMYK** (Cyan, Magenta, Yellow, Black); **HSB** sliders (Hue, Saturation, Brightness); **HSL** sliders (Hue, Saturation, Lightness); **HSL Colour Wheel**; **HSL Colour Box**; or **Greyscale**. models

To set the mode:

- Choose an option from the `RGB ▾` drop-down list.

Defining colours

Now, a few things to remember about how these colours are used:

- When you draw a selection, shape, or use the paintbrush tools, you could apply the foreground colour.

- However, the black text in the design could be created after swapping foreground and background colours using the tab's ⇄ button. Loading the foreground and background colour with two frequently used colours is a great way to boost productivity when painting and drawing.

📌 Why background colour?

When you cut, delete, or erase an area on the Background layer, the area exposes the currently set background colour—as if that colour were there "behind" the portion of the image being removed. (Layers other than the Background layers behave differently: on these, a removed area exposes transparency.)

To define foreground and background colour:

1. Select the **Colour Pickup Tool** on the Tools toolbar.

2. Left-click with the tool anywhere on an image to "pick up" the colour at that point as the new foreground colour. Right-click to define a new background colour.

3. (Optional) On the Context toolbar, set the **Sample Size** (pickup region) as a single "Point Sample", "3 x 3 Average" or "5 x 5 Average" area. The last two options lets you sample an "averaged" colour over a square pixel region, ideal for sampling halftoned images, i.e. when point sampling is not suitable.

> To switch temporarily to the Colour Pickup Tool from a paint, line, shape, fill, or text tool, hold down the **Alt** key, then click to define the foreground colour.

OR

1. On the Colour tab, click and move the mouse pointer (dropper cursor) around the **Colour Spectrum**. As you move the dropper cursor around the spectrum, the tab's active colour swatch updates to the colour at the cursor position.

2. Left-click in the spectrum to set a new foreground colour, and right-click to set a new background colour.

> You can change this RGB spectrum to display in Greyscale, or show the colours spread between the Foreground/Background colours (click the ▽ button on the tab).

OR

•   On the Colour tab, use the slider(s) or enter numeric values in the boxes to define a specific colour. The selected swatch updates instantly.

To swap foreground and background colours, click the ⇅ double arrow button next to the swatches. To reset the colours to black and white, click the black and white mini-swatch at the bottom left of the swatch.

Clicking an active swatch will also let you apply a chosen colour from the Adjust Colour dialog's colour wheel, and will let you define and store that colour in a set of custom colours.

Storing colours

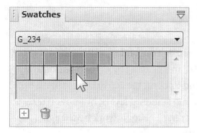

If you want to save colours that you want to work with frequently, you can store them in the Swatches tab as thumbnails (this avoids continually defining colours in the Colour tab). The Swatches tab hosts galleries of categorized colour thumbnails.

If hidden, make this tab visible via **Window>Studio Tabs**.

You can store your currently selected foreground colour (in Colour tab) to the currently selected category (e.g., G_234); you can also create categories yourself into which you can add your own thumbnails. The Swatches tab also lets you choose pre-defined colours from a range of "themed" categories (e.g., Earth, Fruits, Pastel, and web browser safe).

To add a colour to the Swatches tab:

1.   Either:

     Choose a colour from the Colour tab's colour spectrum.

     OR

     Select the **Colour Pickup Tool** and hover over then click on a chosen colour.

     You'll notice the Colour tab's foreground colour swatch change.

2. From the Swatches tab, pick the correct category to store the colour.

3. Click the ⊞ **New Swatch** button to add the foreground colour to the current gallery.

To apply a colour from the Swatches tab:

- Select any gallery thumbnail then paint, draw, fill, etc. Note that a thumbnail click will change the Colour tab's foreground colour.

Painting

The 🖌 **Paintbrush Tool** and ✏ **Pencil Tool** on the Tools toolbar are the basic tools for painting and drawing freehand lines on the active layer. They work on Background and standard layers, but not on text layers or shape layers. The tools work by changing pixels on the layer.

The **Paintbrush Tool** will always apply **anti-aliasing** to its brush strokes without exception. For the most part this is ideal as brush edges will appear very smooth—irrespective of the Hardness setting of your current brush. However, how can a hard-edged brush effect be achieved? This is possible with the **Pencil Tool**, a hard-edged brush tool which is used just like the Paintbrush Tool but always with the hard-edging.

The **Brush Tip tab** hosts a comprehensive collection of brush presets grouped into various categories; each category can be switched to via a drop-down list and displays a gallery. Note that each sample clearly shows the brush tip and stroke; the number indicates the brush diameter. The brush tip determines the thickness and many other properties of the painted line.

💡 You can also create your own brush from within the tab.

If you scroll down the gallery, you'll note that some brushes have hard edges, while others appear fuzzy, with soft edges. The hardness of a brush is expressed as a percentage of its full diameter. If less than 100%, the brush has a soft edge region within which the opacity of applied colour falls off gradually.

Brush attributes (blend mode, opacity, size, and flow) can be modified via a context toolbar (along with more advanced Brush Options) and, if necessary, saved for future use with the Tool Presets tab.

If a more bespoke brush tip is required, you can also customize your own brush tip and save it in its own user-defined category. (See PhotoPlus Help for details.)

An important factor when applying brush strokes is the level of opacity applied to the brush. This attribute affects brush strokes significantly when the stroke is applied onto already transparent standard layers. The greater the opacity the more opaque the brush stroke, and vice versa. Experiment to achieve the right combination of opacity and colour for your brush strokes.

To use the Paintbrush or Pencil tool:

1. From the **Tools** toolbar's **Brush Tools** flyout, select the **Paintbrush Tool** or **Pencil Tool**.

2. Choose a brush tip preset on the Brush Tip tab. If you've picked a Basic brush, set a brush colour (i.e. the foreground colour) from the Colour tab before painting.

3. (Optional) Change brush tip's attributes, if necessary, on the Context toolbar. These changes do not affect the brush presets present in the Brush Tip tab.

4. Drag the cursor on the active layer, holding the left mouse button down to paint in the foreground colour.

Brush options

The Brush Options dialog, accessible from the Context toolbar's **Brush** option, lets you customize a brush or define properties for a new one. As you vary the settings, you can see the effect of each change in the preview window.

Painting using pen tablets

Brush strokes can be applied directly to the page by using your mouse or, if available, a pen tablet; the latter method is ideally suited for applying pressure-sensitive strokes to your project. PhotoPlus supports pressure sensitivity, with tablet calibration and key assignment possible directly from within the program (via Pressure Studio).

Stamping and spraying pictures

The  **Picture Brush Tool** works like a custom brush that sprays a series of pre-defined or custom images at regular intervals as you drag. Used in conjunction with the Brush Tip tab you can select from a variety of picture brushes in different categories, and you can import Paint Shop Pro "picture tubes".

You can use the tool either to "stamp" single images at specific points or lay out a continuous stream of repeating pictures as in the letter "S" on the left.

The Picture Brush tool works on Background and standard layers, but not on text layers or shape layers.

To draw with the Picture Brush:

1. From the **Tools** toolbar's **Brush Tools** flyout, select the Picture Brush Tool.

2. On the Brush Tip tab, pick a brush tip from one of the categories.

    To control image elements, right-click a brush from any Brush Tip tab category, and choose **Brush Options....**

3. From the Context toolbar, scale the opacity and size of the image elements produced by using the **Opacity** and **Diameter** option. For pen tablet users, check stylus **Size** and/or **Opacity** to make these brush properties respond to your pressure device.

4. Note that Diameter isn't an absolute setting, but a relative one. Each picture brush stores its own pre-defined elements, and this scaling determines how the tool scales elements up or down when drawing. The actual size of stored elements varies between brushes, so you may need to adjust the image diameter when switching between different brushes.

5. To "stamp" single images at specific points, click in various places on your canvas. To spray a continuous line of images, drag a path across the page.

To import a Paint Shop Pro picture tube file:

1. On the Brush Tip tab, select a category you've created yourself, right-click and choose **Import...**.

2. Use the dialog to browse for and select the picture tube (.tub) file to import.

If you right-click on any gallery sample, you can manage categories, and access brush options. With a bit of forethought, it's not difficult to lay out your own master images and from them create your own custom Picture Brush tips. (For details, see PhotoPlus Help.)

Erasing

Sometimes the rubber end of the pencil can be just as important to an artist as the pointed one. The Eraser Tools flyout on the Tools toolbar provides ways of enhancing an image by "painting" with transparency rather than with colour:

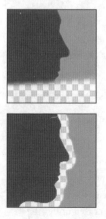

The **Standard Eraser Tool** for replacing colours in an image either with the background colour or with transparency (on Background or other standard layers, respectively).

The **Background Eraser Tool** for erasing pixels similar to a sampled reference colour underlying the cursor crosshair—great for painting out unwanted background colours.

The **Flood Eraser Tool** for filling a region with transparency, erasing pixels similar to the colour under the cursor when you first click.

In general, you can set tool properties for each tool including brush characteristics, opacity, tolerance, flow, and choose a brush tip. The Eraser tools work on Background and standard layers, but not on text layers or shape layers.

To erase with the Standard Eraser:

1. Select **Standard Eraser** from the **Tools** toolbar's **Eraser Tools** flyout.

2. (Optional) Change attributes, especially brush **Size** and **Opacity**, on the Context toolbar.
   For erasing with an airbrush effect or hard-edged brush, check the **Airbrush** or **Hard Edge** option.
   For tablet users, pressure sensitivity can be switched on via Brush Options (click **Brush** thumbnail); ensure the **Controller** drop-down list is set to "Pressure" on selected attributes.

3. Drag with the tool on the active layer. On the Background layer, erased pixels expose the current background colour. On other layers, they expose transparency.

To erase with the Background Eraser:

1. Select **Background Eraser** from the **Tools** toolbar's **Eraser Tools** flyout.

2. (Optional) Change properties on the Context toolbar as described above.

3. Drag with the tool on the active layer to erase pixels similar to a sampled reference colour directly under the brush tip.

   - With "Contiguous" limits (the default), the tool erases only within-tolerance pixels **adjacent** to each other and within the brushes width; this tends to restrict erasure to one side of an edge or line. When you set "Discontiguous" limits, all matching pixels are erased under the brush even if they are non-adjacent (great for removing uniform background like sky). The "Edge Detected" setting can improve erasure along one side of a contrasting edge or line.

Contiguous   Discontiguous

- With "Continual" sampling (the default), the reference colour is repeatedly updated as you move the cursor. Sampling "Once" means erasure is based on the colour under the crosshair when you first click. Use the "Background Swatch" setting to use the current background colour (Colour tab) as the reference.

- You also have the option of protecting the current foreground colour from erasure (**Protect foreground**).

If you use the tool on the Background layer, it's promoted to a standard layer.

To erase with the Flood Eraser:

1. Select **Flood Eraser** from the **Tools** toolbar's **Eraser Tools** flyout.

2. (Optional) Change properties on the Context toolbar.

3. Drag with the tool on the active layer to erase pixels close in colour (based on the Tolerance range) to the colour under the cursor when you first click. If you use the tool on the Background layer, it's promoted to a standard layer.

    - The **Tolerance** setting determines the breadth of the colour range to be erased.

    - The **Opacity** setting will alter the erased areas level of transparency.

- Check **Contiguous** to erase only within-tolerance pixels connected to each other; when unchecked, all in-range pixels are erased.

- Check **Use All Layers** to take colour boundaries on other layers into account, although erasure happens only on the current layer.

- **Anti-alias** smooths the boundary between the erased area and the remaining area.

Erasing using pen tablets

During retouching, areas of your image can be erased by brushing out, either by using your mouse or, if available, a pen tablet. For tablet users, PhotoPlus supports pressure sensitivity, with tablet calibration and key assignment possible directly from within the program (via Pressure Studio).

Using patterns

The  **Pattern Tool** lets you paint a pattern directly onto your canvas. In effect, it "clones" any pattern bitmap you've selected while providing the flexibility to paint wherever you wish, and control opacity, blend mode, and so on. Like the Clone Tool, the Pattern brush picks up pixels from a source—in this case, the bitmap pattern—and deposits them where you're drawing. You can choose a pre-defined, tiled bitmap pattern from the Patterns dialog, or define your own patterns.

As an example, patterns can be used effectively as a painted background, perhaps when creating web graphics.

To paint with a pattern:

1. Select the 🖼 **Pattern Tool** from the **Tools** toolbar's Clone Tools flyout.

2. On the Context toolbar, choose your brush attributes and click the **Pattern** thumbnail to display the Patterns dialog. To select from various pattern categories, right-click any of the thumbnails and choose a different category from the bottom of the flyout menu. Simply click a pattern to select it. Other right-click options let you edit the pattern categories or add new patterns from stored bitmap files.

3. To paint, drag with the tool on the active layer (or in the current selection).

🔖 The **Aligned** check box in the Context toolbar determines what happens each time you begin brushing in a new place. If checked, the pattern extends itself seamlessly with each new brush stroke; if unchecked, it begins again each time you click the mouse.

Creating your own patterns

The built-in selection of patterns in the Patterns dialog provides a useful starting point, but you can also create your own patterns from any selection, or even the whole image. And take a look at the Tile Maker effect if you have a relatively small sample region (like a patch of grass) and want to produce a pattern from it that can be tiled seamlessly over a broader area.

💡 For best results, you'll need to scale your image, or size your selection, so that the pattern is of a suitable size from which to tile from.

To create a new pattern:

1. Define a selection if you wish, and choose **Create Pattern...** from the **Edit** menu.

2. To store the pattern, select a user-defined category from the dialog's **Category** drop-down menu (or keep with the default My Patterns category).

3. Click **OK**.

A thumbnail appears in the category gallery, ready to brush on (or use as a brush tip texture or fill) at any time. Right-clicking any pattern lets you rename the pattern categories or add new patterns from stored bitmap files.

Filling a region

Filling regions or layers is an alternative to brushing on colours or patterns. Making a selection prior to applying a fill, and setting appropriate options, can spell the difference between a humdrum effect and a spectacular one.

The **Fill Tools** flyout on the Tools toolbar includes two tools for filling regions with colour and/or transparency: **Flood Fill** and **Gradient Fill**. In addition, you can use the **Edit>Fill...** command to apply either a **colour** or **pattern** fill. As with paint tools, if there is a selection, the Fill tools only affect pixels within the selected region. If you're operating on a shape or text layer, a single fill affects the interior of the object(s) on the layer.

Flood and pattern fills

The **Flood Fill Tool** works on Background and standard layers, replacing an existing colour region with the foreground colour. How large a region is "flooded" with the fill colour depends on the difference between the colour of the pixel you initially click and the colour of surrounding pixels.

To use the Flood Fill Tool:

1. Select the **Flood Fill Tool** from the **Tools** toolbar's **Fill Tools** flyout.

2. Set tolerance and layer fill options on the Context toolbar.

    - You can use the Context toolbar to set a **tolerance** value—how much of a colour difference the tool looks for. With a low tolerance setting, the tool "gives up easily" and only fills pixels very close in colour to the one you click (a setting of 0 would fill only pixels of the same colour; 255 would fill all pixels). As the tolerance increases, so does the tool's effect on pixels further in colour from the original pixel, so a larger region is flooded.

    - When **Anti-alias** is checked, the boundary of a colour fill is smoothed; uncheck to produce a hard edge to the fill boundary.

    - When checked, **Contiguous** affects only pixels connected to the clicked pixel; uncheck to affect in-range pixels throughout the region.

- The Context toolbar includes an **All Layers** option. If checked, the Flood Fill tool samples pixels on all layers (both shown and hidden) underlying the click point, as if the layers were merged into one. If unchecked, it only samples pixels on the active layer. In either case, it only fills pixels on the active layer.

- A pattern can be applied as a fill from the Context toolbar by picking a **Pattern** (click the thumbnail) from the gallery, then choosing the **Fill** drop down list to be "Pattern".

3. Click with the tool where you want to start the fill.

The **Edit>Fill...** command lets you flood-fill a region on a standard layer using any colour, not just the foreground colour. On the other hand, it's strictly a solid colour flood without the subtleties of the Flood Fill Tool's properties. Simply choose the command to display the Fill dialog.

To use the Fill command:

- Choose **Fill...** from the **Edit** menu. The Fill dialog appears.

- For a flood fill, set the **Type** to Colour.

- Choose whether the fill colour is to be the current **Foreground** colour, **Background** colour or a **Custom** colour.

- Specify the blend mode and opacity of the fill.
  If you check **Preserve Transparency**, transparent areas will resist the flood colour; otherwise, everything in the selection or layer will be equally washed with the fill.

- For a Pattern fill, set the **Type** to **Pattern**.
  The blend options are the same, but in this mode instead of choosing a colour you can fill a region with any pattern stored in the Patterns dialog. Click the pattern sample to bring up the gallery of pattern thumbnails, then right-click any thumbnail to choose a category from the bottom of the list. (See Using patterns on p. 144.)

Gradient Fill Tool

Whereas solid fills use a single colour, all gradient fills in PhotoPlus utilize at least two "key" colours, with a spread of hues in between each key colour, creating a "spectrum" effect. You can fine-tune the actual spread of colour between pairs of key colours. Likewise, a gradient fill in PhotoPlus can have either **solid transparency**—one level of opacity, like 50% or 100%, across its entire range—or **variable transparency**, with at least two "key" opacity levels and a spread of values in between. (Remember that opacity is simply an inverse way of expressing transparency.)

The ⬜ **Gradient Fill Tool** lets you apply variable colour and/or transparency fills directly to a layer. Five types of fill (Solid, Linear, Radial, Conical, and Square) are available. Technically, a Solid fill is different (it uses just one colour) but in practice you can also achieve a unicolour effect using a gradient fill.

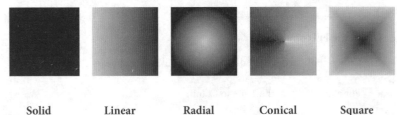

| Solid | Linear | Radial | Conical | Square |

Applying a gradient fill on any kind of layer entails selecting one of the fill types, editing the fill colours and/or transparency in a Gradient dialog, then applying the fill. However, gradient fills behave differently depending on the kind of layer you're working on.

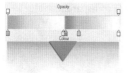

On **standard and Background layers**, the tool creates a "spectrum" effect, filling the active layer or selection with colours spreading between the key colours in the selected gradient fill. The fill is applied rather like a coat of spray paint over existing pixels on the layer; colour and transparency properties in the fill gradient interact with the existing pixels to produce new values. In other words, once you've applied the fill, you can't go back and edit it (except by undoing it and trying again).

Transparency works in a comparable way, affecting how much the paint you apply is "thinned." At full opacity, the fill completely obscures pixels underneath.

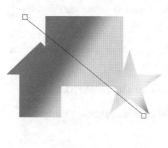

On **text and shape layers**, the Gradient Fill Tool is even more powerful—the fill's colour and transparency properties remain editable. Technically, the fill is a property of the layer, and the shape(s) act as a "window" enabling you to see the fill. Thus a single fill applies to all the shapes on a particular layer—note the gradient fill opposite which is applied across three QuickShapes present on the same layer.

Transparency gradients determine which portions of the object you can see through. Note that the Flood Fill Tool doesn't work with text or shapes. When first drawn, a shape takes a Solid fill using the foreground colour. You can change the fill type as described below.

To apply a gradient fill:

1. Select [ ] **Gradient Fill Tool** from the **Tools** toolbar's **Fill Tools** flyout.

2. Select a fill type from the Context toolbar. Choose Linear, Radial, Conical or Square.

3. To choose a preset or to edit the fill's colours and/or transparency values, click the colour sample on the Context toolbar.

The Gradient dialog appears, where you can select a preset fill from the default gallery or right-click and choose a fill from different pre-defined categories (e.g., Blues, Greens, etc.). The right-click menu also lets you add, edit or delete categories; items can also be added (or deleted) when a custom fill is created in the fill spectrum. See PhotoPlus Help for details on how to edit gradient fills.

4. (Optional) Check **Reverse** to swap the direction of your chosen fill.

5. (Optional) Uncheck **Transparency** if you don't want transparency (if present) in your chosen gradient fill to be preserved; otherwise, the fill's transparency is maintained when the fill is applied.

6. Once you've defined the fill, click with the tool where you want to start the fill and drag to the point where you want it to end.

To change a text or shape layer's fill type, or edit its colour(s):

- Double-click the text/shape layer (or right-click and choose **Edit Fill...**).

    OR

    Choose the **Gradient Fill Tool** and use the Context toolbar.

Either option lets you choose a fill type, and/or click the colour (or gradient) sample to edit the fill.

On text or shape layers, the **fill path** (the line in the illustration above) remains visible even after you've applied the fill, and you can adjust the fill's placement after the fact by dragging the fill path's end nodes with the Gradient Fill Tool.

Cloning a region

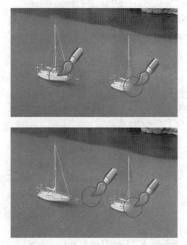

The  **Clone Tool** is like two magic brushes locked together. While you trace or "pick up" an original drawing with one brush, the other draws ("puts down") an exact duplicate somewhere else—even in another image.

When retouching, for example, you can remove an unwanted object from an image by extending another area of the image over it (note the pickup area is positioned over the sea rather than the original boat).

The tool acts on the active Background or standard layer, and can even clone **all** layers (including Text layers or Shape layers).

To clone a region:

1. From the **Tools** toolbar's **Clone Tools** flyout, select the **Clone Tool**.

2. Change properties, if necessary, on the Context toolbar. For example:

    *   Reducing the tool's **Opacity** setting results in a "ghosted" copy of the original pixels.

    *   For additional brush strokes, to always reuse the original pickup point, keep **Aligned** unchecked. Check **Aligned** to have your pickup point change to be offset in relation to your brush tip's position—great for removing unwanted regions that follow a natural path.

Aligned unchecked   *Aligned checked*

- (Optional) For multiple layers, the context toolbar hosts a **Use all layers** option which, when checked, will clone **all** layers (including Background, standard, Text and Shape layers together). When unchecked, only the active (selected) layer is cloned.

3. To define the pickup origin, **Shift**-click with the tool.

4. Click again where you want to start the copy, then drag to paint the copy onto the new location. Repeat as needed. A crosshair marks the pickup point, which moves relative to your brush movements.

Creating and editing text

PhotoPlus makes use of two text tools, i.e.

- The **T** **Text Tool**, for entering solid text on a new layer. Use for eye-catching or subtle captioning (opposite) and titling equally.

- The **T** **Text Selection Tool**, for creating a selection in the shape of text (for filling with unusual fills).

The Layers tab designates **text layers** with a ⊤ symbol. Like shapes, solid text in PhotoPlus is **editable**: as long as it remains on a separate text layer, you can retype it or change its properties at a later date.

To create new solid text:

1. **T · T** Click the **Text Tools** flyout on the **Tools** toolbar and choose the standard **Text Tool**.

2. Click on your image with the text cursor to set where you want to insert text. The text attributes (font, point size, bold/italic/underline, alignment, anti-alias and colour) set on the Text Context toolbar prior to clicking will be applied.

OR

Drag across the page to size your text according to requirements. Release the mouse button to set the point size.

3. Type your text, which is applied directly on your page. The text appears on a new transparent text layer in the image. You can now use the Move Tool or other tools and commands to manipulate it, just like the contents of any layer.

To edit existing text:

1. With the text layer to be edited as the active layer, choose the standard **Text Tool** and move the mouse pointer over the text until it changes to the (I-beam) cursor.

2. Click on or drag to select areas of text—this lets you insert or overwrite selected text, respectively. Equally, you can set new text attributes (font, point size, bold/italic/underline, alignment, anti-alias, or colour) to be adopted by the selected text area—all made from the Text Context toolbar.

> Fine-tune your character size and positioning by using the Character tab. If hidden, make this tab visible via **Window>Studio Tabs**.

To change text's solid colour:

1. Select all or part of any text.

2. Click the colour swatch on the Context toolbar and use the Adjust Colour dialog. (See Choosing colours on p. 134.)

3. Select your new colour and click **OK**.

To swap to a gradient colour:

1. On the **Layers** tab, right-click the Text layer and choose **Edit Fill...**.

2. Change the **Fill Type** from **Solid** to one of Linear, Radial, Conical, or Square.

3. Click on the **Fill** gradient swatch and select a preset gradient fill or create your own gradient from the dialog (see Filling a region on p. 146). The gradient fill is immediately applied to your text.

This applies a gradient fill to all of your text on the layer and not to selected text.

To convert any text layer to a standard layer:

• Right-click on the layer name and choose **Rasterize** from the menu.

To create a text selection:

1. Click the **T** ▾ **Text Tools** flyout (**Tools** toolbar) and choose the 𝕋 **Text Selection Tool**.

2. Click at the location on the image where you want to begin the selection. OR

   Drag across the page to size your text selection according to requirements. Release the mouse button to set the point size.

3. (Optional) On the Text Context toolbar, set the selection text attributes to be adopted by the new selection (e.g., the font and point size).

4. Type your text directly onto the page.

5. When you're done, click the ✅ **OK** button on the Context toolbar. A selection marquee appears around the text's outline.

6. You can now cut, copy, move, modify, and of course fill the selection.

Unlike solid text, the text selection doesn't occupy a separate layer.

Drawing and editing lines and shapes

For drawing and editing lines and shapes, the **Tools** toolbar includes the following drawing tool flyouts:

The **QuickShape Tools** flyout featuring an assortment of tools for creating rectangles, ellipses, polygons, and other shapes.

The **Line Tools** flyout features straight lines, plus freehand pen and curved pen lines.

Overview

Each of the drawing tools has its own creation and editing rules, as detailed below. Before continuing, let's cover some things that all shape objects have in common:

- Shapes have outlines known as **paths**. In a nutshell, shapes as discussed here are **filled** lines (i.e., they're closed, with colour inside). Later, we'll cover **unfilled** lines (paths) separately, and consider their special properties. The various drawing tools are all path-drawing tools, applicable to both the filled and unfilled kind of line.

- Unlike painted regions you create on **raster** (bitmap) layers, both QuickShapes and lines are **vector objects** that occupy special **shape layers**, marked with an ▨ symbol on the Layers tab. Each shape layer includes a path thumbnail representing the shape(s) on that layer.

- A QuickShape or straight line can be drawn directly as a **shape layer**, **path** or as a filled **bitmap**. The Context toolbar hosts buttons which allow you to decide how your lines and shapes are to be drawn, i.e.

  Shape Layer—create your QuickShape or line on a new shape layer or add to an existing shape layer.

  Paths—add your shape or line directly as a path rather than as a new/existing shape layer. (See Using paths on p. 163).

  Fill Bitmaps—creates a filled bitmap of the shape or straight line on a raster layer (e.g., the Background layer).

Curved and freehand pen lines cannot be drawn as filled bitmaps.

Assuming you're working on a non-shape layer when you create a shape, the new shape appears on a new shape layer. But what about the next shape you create? Shape layers can store more than one shape, and it's up to you where the next one will go.

This decision is made easy by use of the Context toolbar when the QuickShape or line tool is selected. The toolbar displays a series of **combination buttons** which determine the layer on which the shape will be placed and the relationship the new shape will have on any existing shapes on the same layer.

New—Adds the shape to a new shape layer.

Add—Adds the shape to the currently selected layer.

Subtract—removes overlap region when a new shape is added over existing shapes on the currently selected layer. The new shape itself is not included.

Intersect—includes the intersection area only when a new shape is added onto existing selected shapes on the currently selected layer.

Exclude—excludes the intersection area when a new shape is added onto existing selected shapes on the currently selected layer.

To change the fill type, or edit its colour(s):

- Double-click the shape layer.

    OR

    Choose the Gradient Fill Tool and use the Context toolbar.

    Either approach lets you add a spectrum fill, a solid colour fill, and/or a transparency gradient to a shape or text object.

- A single fill is shared by all the shapes on a particular layer. (Technically the fill is a property of the layer, and the shape(s) act like a "window" that lets you see the fill.) So if you want to draw a red box and a yellow box, for example, you'll need two shape layers.

You can also alter a shape layer's **Opacity** using the Layers tab.

Creating and editing QuickShapes

QuickShapes in PhotoPlus are pre-designed, filled contours that let you instantly add all kinds of shapes to your page, then adjust and vary them using control handles—for innumerable possibilities!

The **QuickShape Tools** flyout lets you choose from a wide variety of commonly used shapes, including boxes, ovals, arrows, polygons, stars, and more. Each shape has its own built-in "intelligent" properties, which you can use to customize the basic shape.

QuickShapes can also be drawn as paths as described elsewhere in Using paths (see p. 163).

To create a QuickShape :

1. Click the ⬜▾ **QuickShapes** flyout on the **Tools** Toolbar and select a shape from the flyout menu. (To choose the most recently used shape, just click the toolbar button directly.)

2. Ensure the ⬚ **Shape Layers** button is selected on the Context toolbar.

3. If creating the shape on a new layer, make sure the ⬜ **New** button on the Context toolbar is selected. If creating multiple shapes on the same layer, select one of the other combination buttons on the Context Bar (see above) to specify how the multiple shapes will interact (see above).

4. Select a foreground colour, and any other characteristics for the QuickShape.

5. Drag out the shape on the image. It displays as an outline; hold down the **Ctrl** key while drawing to constrain the aspect ratio. Once drawn, the shape takes a Solid fill using the Colour tab's foreground colour.

> To create a filled bitmap from your QuickShape instead, choose the ⬜ **Fill Bitmaps** button instead of the **Shape Layers** button.

Each QuickShape is adjustable, so you can experiment before committing to a particular figure and edit it later—with innumerable possibilities!

If you switch to the **Node Edit Tool**, you can adjust the shape. The number of displayed "edit" control handles varies according to the shape; for example, the rectangle has just one control, the polygon has two, and the star has four.

As an example, dragging the side control handle on the middle Quick Pentagon shape downwards will morph the shape to a hexagon, heptagon, octagon, and so on. Dragging the top control handle to the right will rotate the shape in an anti-clockwise direction.

To edit a QuickShape:

1. Click its layer or path name in the Layers or Paths tab, respectively, to select it. If on a Shape layer, make sure the layer's path thumbnail is **selected** (it has a white border; arrowed below) to allow the path to be edited with the Node Edit Tool or Shape Edit Tool, i.e.

2. Use either:

   - The ⯈ **Node Edit Tool** (**Tools** toolbar) to click on the shape and readjust any of the shape's handles.

     OR

   - The ⬚⬈ **Shape Edit Tool** to select, move, resize, and deform individual shapes.

     (If you only have one shape on a layer, you can use the **Move Tool** and **Deform Tool**.) To resize without constraint, you can drag any shape's handle; to constrain the shape's proportions, hold down the **Shift** key while dragging. To deform the shape, drag a node while the **Ctrl** key is pressed.

Creating and editing lines

Lines can be drawn by using dedicated tools from the **Tools** toolbar's Line Tools flyout.

The **Line Tool** produces an anti-aliased straight line in PhotoPlus, which is just a very thin shape. The line can be of varying **Weight** (thickness) and can be constrained to 15-degree increments, by holding down the **Shift** key as you drag.

The **Freehand Pen Tool**, as its name implies, lets you draw a squiggly line made up of consecutive line segments and nodes (each new segment starting from another's end node), which can be attached back to itself to create a closed shape. Use the **Smoothness** setting on the Context toolbar to even out ragged contours automatically.

The **Pen Tool** can produce complex combination curves (and shapes) in a highly controlled way.

Each tool's supporting context toolbar lets you create the line on a shape layer, as a path or directly as a filled bitmap. Additionally, combination buttons let you add the line to its own layer (or path), and can also be used to control how the new line interacts with existing shapes on the layer.

Besides being useful with QuickShapes, the Node Edit and Shape Edit tools really come into their own when editing lines.

To edit a line:

1. Click its layer name to select the layer.

2. To move, resize, scale, skew, or rotate the line, choose the **Shape Edit Tool**. This deform tool works by manipulation of the bounding box around the line—drag on a corner or edge. (For details on its use, see Deforming on p. 117.)

3. To reshape the line, choose the △ **Node Edit Tool**. The line consists of **line segments** and **nodes** (points where the line segments meet). You can drag one or more individual nodes, or click and drag directly on a line segment.

When you select a node, control handles for the adjacent line segments appear; each segment in the line has a control handle at either end. The selected node is drawn with a red centre, with the control handle(s) attached to the nodes by blue lines.

Any node can be one of several node types: **sharp**, **smooth**, or **symmetric**. Depending on node type, the node's control handles behave a bit differently, as you can tell with a bit of experimentation. Essentially, the node type determines the slope and curvature of each adjoining segment, and can be chosen from the Context toolbar, i.e.

⌢ **Sharp Corner** means that the segments either side of the node are completely independent so that the corner can be quite pointed.

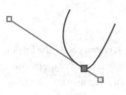

⌢ **Smooth Corner** means that the slope of the line is the same on both sides of the node, but the depth of the two joined segments can be different.

⌢ **Symmetric Corner** nodes join line segments with the same slope and depth on both sides of the node.

To edit a node:

1. Select it with the Node Edit Tool.

2. Drag its control handle(s) to fine-tune the curve.

You can also use the context toolbar to define a line segment as either straight or curved.

To add a node, double-click on a line segment. To remove a selected node, press the **Delete** key.

> ✦ Use the ⌐ **Straighten Line** button to make an line segment straight.

Creating outlines

Two approaches to creating outlines are available within PhotoPlus—creating an outline from any current **selection** and creating outlines around layer objects, especially text and shapes (as a **layer effect**). You'll primarily create outlines around text and other objects so the latter method is predominantly used (but we'll cover both!).

Selection
(before and after)

Text
(before and after)

For any outline, you can set the outline width, solid colour, opacity, and choose a blend mode. The outline can also sit inside, outside, or be centred on the selection or object edge.

An outline layer effect can also take a gradient fill, a pattern fill, or a unique **contour** fill (fill runs from the inner to outer edge of the outline width); another advantage over outlines made from selections is the ability to switch the layer object outline off/on, and complement the outline with other layer effects such as Drop Shadow, Glow, Bevel, etc. at the same time.

To create an outline from a selection:

1. Create a selection on a standard or background layer (but not on Text or Shape layers). (See Making a selection on p. 97).

2. Select **Outline...** from the **Edit** menu.

3. From the dialog, choose a **Width** for the outline.

4. Select an outline colour from the drop-down list. The **Foreground** option sets the currently set foreground colour; **Background** sets the current background colour. (See Choosing colours on p. 134). For a **Custom** colour, click the Colour swatch, and select a colour from the displayed Adjust Colour dialog.

5. (Optional) From the **Mode** drop-down menu, pick a blend mode, which controls how the outline colour and underlying pixels blend to make a combined resulting colour. Select the percentage **Opacity** for the outline when blending, and check **Preserve Transparency** to make transparent areas resist the flood colour; otherwise, everything in the selection or layer will be equally washed with the fill.

6. Click **OK**. The outline appears around the selection area.

Once applied, selection outlines no longer remain editable, although if you're not happy with your outline you can still Undo.

To create outlines on a layer (as a layer effect):

1. From the Layers tab, select a layer to which outlines will be applied. Note that all objects (Shapes, Text, or lines) on the layer will be affected.

2. Click the *fx* **Layer Effects** button on the Layers tab and check **Outline** in the Layer Effects dialog.

3. (Optional) From the **Blend Mode** drop-down menu, pick a blend mode, which controls how the outline colour and underlying pixels blend to make a combined resulting colour. Select the percentage **Opacity** for the outline when blending.

4. Choose a **Width** for the outline, and whether the outline **Alignment** is "Outside" or "Inside" the object's edge (or placed in the "Centre").

5. To set a fill for your outline, pick from the **Fill type** drop-down menu, one of: **Solid**, **Linear**, **Radial**, **Conical**, **Square**, **Contour**, or **Pattern**. Choosing **Solid** will display a colour swatch which, when clicked, shows the **Adjust Colour** dialog. For other fills, click the gradient fill swatch and apply/edit your gradient fill accordingly (see Editing a gradient fill in PhotoPlus Help for details). Pattern fills can be applied via a clickable Pattern swatch (see Using patterns on p. 144 for details).

6. Click **OK**. The outline appears around any layer object.

You may notice the *fx* icon appear next to the layer with your outline applied.

Remember that you'll be able to apply a combination of 2D layer effects along with your outline, by checking other options in the Layer Effects dialog.

To switch off the layer effect:

- With the layer selected, click the *fx* **Layer Effects** button and uncheck **Outline** in the Layer Effects dialog.

Using paths

Paths are basically outlines. As such, every filled shape you draw has a path—namely the outline that defines it. In fact, each shape layer has its own path thumbnail next to the layer name, representing the shape(s) that reside on that layer. But more significantly, the concept of a path extends to **independent paths**: unfilled outlines that don't reside on any particular layer, but which are created separately and can be applied in various ways to any layer.

What are paths good for? Consider the precision and editability of vector-based drawing and apply it to the concept of a selection. Now think of all the ways that selections can be used (and reused). In PhotoPlus, selections and paths are interchangeable.

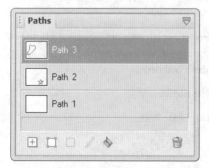

In much the same way as layers in the Layers tab, independent paths are listed in the Paths tab, depicted with their own name and the **path outline** shown in the path's thumbnail.

If hidden, make this tab visible via **Window>Studio Tabs**.

There are two methods for creating a path. You can create:

- a path outline directly from drawn QuickShapes (see Path 2's Quick Star above) or outlines.

- a selection on your image from which the path outline can be created (see Path 3).

Either way, once you've got a path outline, you can reshape it (using the Outline tools), convert it to a selection, create a filled bitmap, or **stroke** a path—that is, draw the path onto a bitmap layer using the current brush. Paths are saved along with the image when you use the SPP format.

To create a path outline from a QuickShape/outline or selection:

1. Select a QuickShape or Outline tool, then ensure **Paths** is selected on the Context toolbar. (For details on using these tools, see Drawing and editing lines and shapes on p. 154).

2. Drag across the page to create your path.

   OR

1. To create a path outline whose shape matches any selection area, first create the selection on a layer.

2. Click **Selection to Path** on the Paths tab.

3. In the dialog, choose a **Smoothness** setting (to even out jagged selections) and click **OK**. The new path outline appears on a new path with a default name (which you can change, as described below).

To duplicate the selected path and its outline:

- Right-click its name and choose **Duplicate Path**.

To delete the selected path:

- Click the Path tab's **Delete Path** button**Delete Path**.

To rename the selected path:

1. Double-click its name**Rename Path...**.

2. In the dialog, type a new name for the path.

To edit a path outline:

- Use the **Node Edit Tool** to modify a path's shape by moving nodes or adjust outline curves by moving node handles.

- Use the **Shape Edit Tool** to move, resize, reshape, rotate, and skew the path by dragging the displayed bounding box handles in any direction.

For both methods, see Creating and editing outline shapes on p. 161 for more details.

You can also flip a path outline either horizontally or vertically. Use the **Flip Horizontally>Path** or **Flip Vertically>Path** option from the **Image** menu, respectively.

To create a selection from a path:

1. Select the Background or standard layer where you want to create the selection.

2. On the Paths tab, select the path from which you want to create the selection.

3. Click the [ ] **Path to Selection** button (or right-click the path entry).

4. In the dialog, set options for the selection:

   - The **Feather** value blurs the selection's edges by making edge pixels semi-transparent.

   - Check **Anti-alias** to produce smooth edges by softening the colour transition between edge pixels and background pixels.

   - Select **New Selection**, **Add to Selection**, **Subtract from Selection**, or **Intersect with Selection** to determine how the path-based selection should interact with an existing selection, if any.

5. Click **OK**. The selection marquee appears on the target layer.

To draw (stroke) a path onto a bitmap layer:

1. Select the Background or standard layer where you want to add the bitmap.

2. Choose a brush tool (such as the Paintbrush or Picture Brush) and set Colour, Brush Tip, and other properties from the Context toolbar.

3. On the Paths tab, select the path you want to stroke. Make sure the path is positioned where you want it.

4. Click the   **Stroke Path** button.

To create a filled bitmap from a path:

1. Select the Background or standard layer where you want to create the filled bitmap.

2. Set a foreground colour.

3. On the Paths tab, select the path you want to fill. Make sure the path is positioned where you want it.

4. Click the   **Fill Path** button (or right-click the path and choose **Fill Path**).

7 Making Images for the Web

Slicing images

Image slicing and **image maps** are two convenient ways to create navigation bars and clickable graphics for web pages. With image slicing, a graphic is carved up into smaller graphics—each of which can have its own link, like any web graphic—and PhotoPlus saves the sections as separate files when you export the image. The process also exports HTML tags describing a table containing the separate graphics, allowing a web browser to reassemble them seamlessly. The result appears as a single larger graphic, but with different regions linked to different targets.

For example, the menubar graphic (below top)... can be sliced into four separate graphics (below bottom), each linked to a different web page.

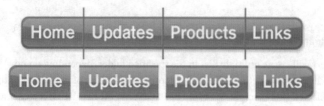

The Image Slice Tool lets you divide the image into sections which can be exported to the GIF or JPG file format. You can specify alternate text and URL links for each of the image sections individually.

To slice the image:

- Choose the **Image Slice Tool** from the **Standard** toolbar.

- To place a horizontal slice guide on the image, click on the image at your chosen cursor position. **Shift**-click to place a vertical guide. A guide line appears with each click.

- To move a guide, simply drag it.

- To delete a guide, drag it out of the image window.

To specify the alternate text and/or link:

• Right-click an image slice (any area enclosed by horizontal and vertical slice guides) and enter the alternate **Text** and **URL** (link) information in the dialog.

Once you've sliced up your image you have to export it to make the image slices understandable to a web visitor's browser.

To export a sliced image:

• When exporting with **File>Export Optimizer**, specify a name and folder for the files as usual, and choose either GIF or JPG as the export file type. Ensure the **Create Image Slices** box is checked on the second Export dialog.

Since exporting slices creates multiple files, you may wish to create a separate folder for them.

The export will create multiple files in the specified folder, depending on how many slices you have defined. The output consists of a series of image files of the format selected (for example, MYFILEH0V0.GIF, MYFILEH0V1.GIF, etc.) and a single HTML file (for example, MYFILE.HTM). The HTML file contains the tags for the set of image slices, ready to be pasted into the source code for the web page.

Creating image maps

Image maps consist of **hotspots** that you draw with special tools over selected parts of an image. When a visitor passes their mouse cursor over the hotspot, a small caption is displayed and the pointer will change to a pointing hand. Clicking the mouse while the cursor is over the hotspot will invoke a hyperlink to a specified URL.

You assign each hotspot its own target—for example, the URL of a web page. Hotspots aren't attached to a particular image, but become part of a larger "map" that gets exported (p. 172) along with an image and turns into HTML code. It's then up to the web developer to embed the image map code properly into the web page.

Image maps are useful if you want to define isolated and/or irregularly shaped clickable regions on a web graphic, as opposed to subdividing the entire graphic into rectangular image slices.

To draw a hotspot:

1. Click the **Image Map Tools** flyout on the **Standard** toolbar and choose one of the following tools:

   Image Map Rectangle

   Image Map Circle

   Image Map Polygon

2. For rectangles and circles, use the tool to drag out a hotspot on the active layer. To draw a polygon, drag and release the mouse button to define each line segment; double-click to close the polygon. All hotspots are shaded in turquoise.

When using the **Image Map Rectangle**, hold down the **Ctrl** key while dragging out to constrain the hotspot's shape to a square.

To edit a hotspot:

1. Click the **Image Map Tools** flyout and choose the ⬉ **Image Map Selection** tool.

2. Select your hotspot on the page, which then offers you several editing options.

   - To resize the hotspot, drag the displayed square nodes.

   - To move the hotspot, drag from the centre.

   - Right-click the hotspot to set hotspot **Properties...**. Enter hover-over **Text** and add an associated target **URL**. Previously used URLs are saved and can be selected from the drop-down list by clicking on the arrow at the end of the box. On export, entered text will pop up when the cursor moves over the hotspot.

The right-click menu also lets you order overlapping hotspots and to **Delete** selected hotspots.

To export an image map:

- When exporting via Export Optimizer, export the image for which you have created the image map as a GIF (for non-photographic images) or a JPG (for photographic images). Ensure the **Create HTML for Image Maps** box is checked on the second Export dialog.

The output consists of an image file and an HTML file with the same base name. The HTML file contains the tags for the image map, ready to be pasted into the source code for the web page.

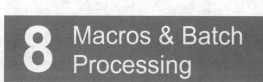

8 Macros & Batch Processing

Understanding macros

If there are operations that you want to repeatedly perform in PhotoPlus, you can apply a **macro**. Put simply, a macro is a saved sequence of commands that can be stored and then recalled at a later date. Macros can be used for:

- Downsampling

- Reformatting

- Applying effects

- Applying adjustments

- Framing and vignetting

PhotoPlus offers a wide range of pre-recorded macros ready for your use. These macros are available in the Macros tab, where they are separated into various categories including Black & White Photography, Colour, Commands, Vignettes, Layout Blurs, and Frames to name but a few.

You'll notice an ▷ icon next to each macro which, when clicked, displays the commands that make up the macro (click to collapse again). For example, a macro that creates a wood frame would have a series of recorded commands listed chronologically. They may be enabled, disabled, reordered or made interactive "on the fly".

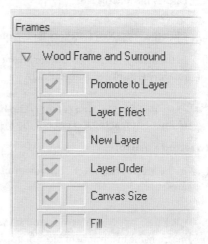

You can cut, copy, paste or even duplicate any macro. This allows you to modify preset macros once pasted into your own user-defined categories.

Recording Macros

Of course at some point you may want to record your own macro. It's probably a good idea to create a new category into which you can save your newly recorded macros—this keeps them separate from the pre-recorded macros supplied with PhotoPlus. This is because recorded macros will be indistinguishable from your preset macros once recorded.

When recording macros, it can be a good idea to ensure that the Layout Rulers/Grid units in **File>Preferences** are set to "percent". This approach ensures that recorded macro commands such as document resizing or framing are carried out in proportion to the original photo rather than by an absolute value. Imagine adding an absolute frame size to a small photo that would otherwise be acceptable on the larger photo. On some occasions you may want to use absolute values—simply use absolute grid units.

Try to plan ahead before recording—If you jot down your intended command sequence you'll make fewer mistakes!

To create a new category:

1. Display the **Macros** tab.

2. Click the **New Category** button on the Macros tab.

3. In the dialog, enter a new category name and click **OK**. The new empty category is displayed automatically.

Any currently displayed category can be edited or deleted via the ▽ **Tab Menu** button at the top right of the Macros tab.

To record a macro:

1. In the **Macros** tab, select a category from the drop-down list of category names.

2. Click the **New Macro** button at the bottom of the Macros tab, enter a macro name in advance of recording your macro, then click **OK**. The

macro name appears at the bottom of the list of macros in the currently displayed category.

3. Select the ○ **Start Recording** button. Any command that can be saved in a macro will be stored while recording is in progress.

4. Carry out the command sequence you want to record, following the instructions when necessary.

5. Stop recording your macro with the ▢ **Stop Recording** button!

To view the macro, navigate to the correct category, then click on the ▷ icon to expand the entry to show the command list recorded by the macro.

Playing Macros

To play a macro you need to choose a photo to which you want to apply the preset or custom macro you've just recorded. Any macro needs to be played to repeat the recorded commands.

To play a macro:

1. Open the photo you wish to apply the macro to.

2. From the **Macros** tab, choose a category from the drop-down menu, then select your macro.

3. Choose the ▷ **Play** button to play the macro.

> Abort any macro playback at any time with the **ESC** key.

Modifying Macros

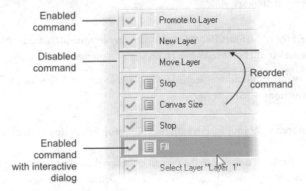

Once you've recorded and played back your macro it's possible to modify the macro's saved sequence of commands. These are listed in the order they were recorded and may be enabled, disabled, reordered or made interactive "on the fly". Macro commands are enabled by default.

In the command list, the command order can be rearranged by simple drag and drop of any command into a new position.

For custom macros you've created yourself, it is also possible to perform a right-click to delete, rename or duplicate a command from the flyout menu.

Any changes made will be applied to the macro immediately such that no file saving is required.

> It is possible to copy and paste preset macros to any user-defined category but not individual commands within each macro.

> If you significantly modify your macro command list your macro may become unusable, so it's important to exercise some restraint while editing—experimentation and testing is the rule of thumb.

To switch a command off:

1. Click the ▷ icon next to the macro name to reveal the macro's command list in the drop-down menu.

2. Each list entry begins with a check box which switches on or off the relevant command. Uncheck the box to switch the command off.

> Experimentation is required when switching commands on or off—some
> commands are integral to the way a macro operates!

To enable command interactivity:

This allows you to intervene in the macro running process to alter some dialog
values, i.e. the next time a macro is played, the macro will pop-up the relevant
dialog associated with a command, pausing the macro temporarily. For example,
for a "Frames" macro, the **Fill** dialog could be made to display during macro
playback to allow a new fill to be entered manually (try some preset Frames
macros + options for examples of this).

1.   Click the empty box before a command name to display
      the **Enable\Disable Dialog** icon.

2.   Load a photo and play the modified macro. The macro pauses to display a
      dialog associated with the above command name.

3.   Modify any settings and press the **OK** button. The macro will continue.

To switch off command interactivity, simply click the icon again.

> Did you spot that some commands have no "interactive" boxes? This is
> because some commands by their nature have no dialogs associated
> with them!

To add manual instructions to your command list:

Another example of interactivity is the inclusion of a pause into any **custom**
macro. This allows you to pop up manual instructions (or important notes) in a
dialog at pre-defined points as your macro runs. There are a number of reasons
for doing this—your macro can't record selections or operations that are
particular to each photo so manual selection is essential in some instances, or
maybe you want to add a helpful note (e.g., "perform a brush stroke") or warning
in advance of a required action or dialog.

1.   Right-click on a command in a custom macro's command list and select
      Insert Pause... from the flyout menu.

2.   Add some relevant notes into the **Stop Options** dialog—check **Allow
      continue** if you want to present a **Continue** button in your dialog as the
      macro runs. Clicking the button will continue the macro process.

3. Click **OK**. The **Stop** command is added to the command list below the command you performed a right-click on (you may want to drag it to before the command).

4. Load a photo and play the modified macro (see **Playing Macros**). The macro pauses to display a dialog with your instructions—remember these before the next step!

5. Click the **Stop** button.

6. Perform the task(s) as instructed in the dialog.

7. Press the ▷ button to continue the macro from the next command in the list after the **Stop** command.

> If you don't need to perform the manual operation, click **Continue** to continue the macro without pausing.

Copying, duplicating and deleting Macros

With the vast collection of macros and commands at your disposal, it's useful to know that you can copy/paste any preset macros to any user-defined category for modification—simply right-click on the macro to be copied and select **Copy**. You can paste the macro by right-click then selecting **Paste** (the macro will be added to the end of the category list). Additionally, commands can be moved (as opposed to copied) between any user-defined macros by drag and drop.

> You can't copy macros or commands into any preset category.

User-defined macros and their associated commands can also be duplicated (or deleted) by right-click and selection of the **Duplicate** (or **Delete**) command.

Batch processing

The batch processing feature is especially useful if you want to repeat the same operation again and again... Batch processing allows you to:

*   Use Macros: uses preset or custom macros as part of the batch process.

*   Change File Type: to bulk convert images to a new file type (with different file properties if needed).

- Resize Images: to resample images to various widths, heights, or resolutions (using different resampling methods).

- Change File Name: to alter the file names of images in bulk.

For any of the above, you specify separate source and destination folders as your input and output. There are several advantages to this, mainly that your original photos are not overwritten.

The **Batch** dialog, available from the **File** menu, is used to perform all of the above operations.

As a pre-requisite, you have to define a specific **Source Folder** for any batch processing operation, whether using a macro or not, or if converting photos to a different file format.

A **Destination folder** can optionally be defined, creating new files in that new location.

⚠ If you don't select a destination folder, the source files will be processed and your original files will be overwritten—exercise caution with these settings!

To save you time, PhotoPlus will remember previously selected Source and Destination folders while PhotoPlus is loaded.

You may be wondering how batch processing affects photos currently loaded in PhotoPlus. PhotoPlus's batch processing only operates on source folder contents and not on the currently loaded photos themselves—so these remain unaffected. However, as a visual check, you will see each photo temporarily being loaded and converted one-by-one in the Photo window during batch processing.

Check the output folder via Windows Explorer to ensure the results are as you expect.

Using macros

Macros (see p. 173) can be applied to a batch process easily (via **Use Macros**). PhotoPlus doesn't differentiate between pre-recorded and recorded macros. If available, they are selected from the same **Category** and **Macro** drop-down menus equally.

Changing file type

It is possible to convert your photos into one of many different file types available in PhotoPlus (via **Change File Type**). In addition, conversion options such as bit depth, palette, dithering, compression/quality, and matte can be selected depending on the file type.

File conversions can be carried out independently or in conjunction with macros (the dialogs shown opposite converts each image to 24-bit PNG format).

Changing image size

As well as changing file formats, PhotoPlus can use batch processing to alter image sizes in bulk (using a choice of resampling methods) via **Resize Images**. Typically, this is a quick and easy way to make your images scale to a maximum image dimension (height or width) with aspect ratio maintained, to absolute image dimensions (with stretching/shrinking to fit), scale by percentage, and scale by resolution (DPI). Use for sending your digital photos via email or perhaps to publish your images online via a website.

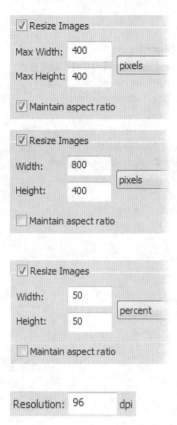

- Check **Maintain aspect ratio** then enter values for **Max Width** and **Max Height** to scale to maximum intended dimensions while preserving the image's original aspect ratio.

- With **Maintain aspect ratio** unchecked, enter values for absolute **Width** and **Height** to make images of a fixed size. As aspect ratio is not maintained, images may be stretched horizontally or vertically.

- Change the units of measurement to percent, then enter identical percentage values to scale **Width** and **Height** in proportion (maintain aspect ratio); otherwise, different values will stretch images horizontally or vertically.

- Enter a DPI value to alter the original resolution of the images.

Resampling Method

- Pick a method from the drop-down list. Use Nearest Pixel for hard-edge images, Bilinear Interpolation when shrinking photos, Bicubic Interpolation when enlarging photos, and Lanczos3 Window when best quality results are expected. The list is ordered according to processing times (fastest to slowest).

Changing file names

It is also possible to define a Destination **File Name** for the files to be processed by selecting the dialog's **Modify...** button. In the **File Name Format** dialog you can select new file names that can be built up using the current date/time, document names, sequence number, or text string, individually or in combination.

⚠ Use the sequence number to generate a separate file for every file to be converted—otherwise your first converted file will be overwritten continually!

9 Creating Animations

Getting started with animation

Animation creates an illusion of motion or change by displaying a series of still pictures, rapidly enough to fool the eye—or more accurately, the brain. With PhotoPlus, it's easy to create and edit images with multiple frames, then export them as **animated GIFs** that a web browser can play back, or **AVI movies** for multimedia applications. You use exactly the same tools and interface as for creating standard, multi-layer PhotoPlus images, with an extra tab, the Animation tab, that includes all the additional controls you need to set up frames, add special effects, and preview the animation. Once you're satisfied, use the Export Optimizer to output to Animated GIF or AVI movie.

PhotoPlus gives you the choice of creating your animations from scratch, importing a GIF or AVI file to edit, or converting existing photos to an animation by selecting **Convert to Animation** from the **File** menu. Either way, once PhotoPlus detects an animation file, it switches on the Animation tab. If the image file is new, you'll see a single, blank frame, labelled "Frame 1." If you've imported an animation, the tab displays each frame separately. Animation files can have one layer, or many, but all their layers are standard (transparent) layers; there's no Background layer. If a photo is used, the first frame will be the photo image.

> The Animation tab only displays when an animation is currently open.

Layers and frames

Animations are created in the **Animation tab** (docked next to the Documents tab at the bottom of your workspace) which works in conjunction with the **Layers tab**. The tab displays a sequence of frame thumbnails. Each frame is a different state of the image, defined in terms of which layers are shown or hidden, the position of content on each shown layer, and the opacity of each shown layer.

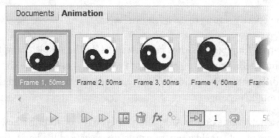

In this file (as in any imported GIF animation) the individual frames can each occupy one layer in the PhotoPlus image. This is controlled with the **Add Layer to Each New Frame** check box, available by right-clicking the Animation tab. Each new frame can therefore be edited independently as it occupies its own layer.

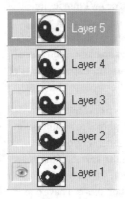

On the Layers tab, the layer stack for this animation corresponds with the frame sequence, with default names—in this case, the default "Layer 1" through to "Layer 5". You'll notice the thumbnails correlate between frame and layer.

If you select Frame 1 on the Animation tab (above), you'll see that on the Layers tab (left) only the "Layer 1" layer is marked as shown, with an open-eye button; the other layers are all hidden.

If you then select Frame 2, the "Layer 2" layer will be shown, with all those above remaining hidden. And so on with the other frames.

The above example, with its one-to-one correspondence between frames and layers, is easy to grasp—but don't make the mistake of thinking that a "frame" is just another name for a "layer." Frames in PhotoPlus are actually much more versatile!

Key point: A so-called "frame" is really just a particular state or snapshot of the various layers in the image, in terms of three layer properties:

- **Shown/Hidden:** Which layers are shown and which are hidden

- **Position:** The position of the contents of each "shown" layer

- **Opacity:** The opacity setting of each "shown" layer

As you switch between frames, you switch between states. In the simple example above, the six frames define six states in terms of Property 1—each of the six frames defines a different layer as "shown." We could rename the layers and the animation itself wouldn't change.

When you create a new frame on the Animation tab, you're not adding a new layer. The new frame merely enables you to define a new state of the layers that already exist. Of course, you could go on and create an additional layer (using the Layers tab), but then all your animation frames would need to take that layer into account—in other words, hide it when it wasn't needed.

Single-layer animation

Let's look at a different example (below) which shows the Yin-Yang symbol as a bouncing ball, and although it has four frames it only has one layer (Add Layer to Each New Frame was unchecked). Three additional frames were cloned from Frame 1 (using the **New Frame** button), and then, within each subsequent frame the layer was dragged slightly (with the Move Tool) to reposition its contents in the window.

Frame 1, 200ms   Frame 2, 200ms   Frame 3, 200ms   Frame 4, 200ms

Working with animation frames

Let's cover the "nuts and bolts" of creating and arranging animation frames using the Animation tab. You'll use the tab in conjunction with the Layers tab to varying extents, but we'll focus on the Animation tab for the moment.

Here are some general guidelines to help you produce memorable animations:

1. Decide if you want layers to be created with each frame. Check or uncheck the **Add Layer to Each New Frame** option (if needed) by right-clicking on the Animation tab. This means that each new frame can be edited independently as it occupies its own layer.

2. Create enough frames to define the separate states of the animation.

3. Step through the frames, adjusting layer content and state for each frame. You can delete or reposition frames as needed, and preview the animation at any time.

4. Save the animation as a regular PhotoPlus (.spp) file, and export it to the GIF or AVI format.

To create a new frame:

- Click the ⊞ **New Frame** button (or right-click a thumbnail and choose **New Frame**).

The previously selected frame is cloned as a new frame, immediately following it in the sequence.

To select a single frame:

- To select any one frame, click its thumbnail.

- Click the ◁ **First Frame** button to select the first frame of the sequence (rewind).

- Click the ◁ **Previous Frame** button to select the previous frame of the sequence.
  If the first frame was selected, you'll cycle back to the last frame of the sequence.

- Click the ▷ **Next Frame** button to select the next frame of the sequence. If the last frame of the sequence was selected, you'll cycle forward to the first frame.

- Click the ▷ **Last Frame** button to select the last frame of the sequence.

To select more than one frame:

- To select multiple non-adjacent frames, hold down the **Ctrl** key when selecting each one.

- To select a range of adjacent frames, hold down the **Shift** key and click the first and last thumbnail in the range.

To make the animation process more efficient:

- ⚬ **Tweening**, short for "in-betweening", automatically creates a chosen number of frames between the currently selected frame and the previous or next frame. This gives a smoother transition of your animation during playback and saves you time. Click to launch the Tween dialog.

  - Set the number of new frames to be created between the next and previous frames.

  - Apply the tweening to just the currently selected layer or all layers.

  - Set which frame attributes are to be tweened—choose Position, Opacity and/or Effects. Position lets you distribute frame objects evenly between next and previous frames (great for creating motion quickly).

- To clone multiple frames, select (see above) then click the **New Frame** button. To clone all frames, right-click the tab and choose **Select All** then clone.

- Use **Reverse Frames** on the right-click menu to reverse the order of a series of selected frames. For example, for bouncing ball animations, create the animated ball as if it were being dropped, use the above "clone all frame" technique on all frames, then reverse the newly cloned frames while selected. You may need to remove the first of the cloned frames because of duplication.

To mirror a frame layer's attributes:

- To mirror the attributes of a frame's layers with respect to Position, Opacity, Blend Mode, Visibility and Effects, select specific or all frames (see above) ensuring that the "target" frame which possesses the attribute(s) to be copied is selected **first**, then choose **Unify Layer Across Frames**. All "destination" frames adopt the layer attributes of the "target" frame.

To delete one or more frames:

- Select the thumbnail(s) and click the 🗑 **Delete Frame** button. (To delete a single frame, you can also right-click it and choose **Delete**.)

To reposition a frame in the sequence:

- Drag its thumbnail and drop it before or after another frame. Note the black vertical insertion cursor to indicate the proposed new position of a frame.

To play (preview) the animation:

- Click the ▷ **Play** button.

The Animation tab includes two options—one global, the other local—that you should consider before exporting the animation.

- For GIF (not AVI files), you can set a **loop** property for the animation as a whole. (You can also set this property on the Animation pane of the Export Optimizer.)

  If you want the sequence to play through only once and end displaying the first frame, click the **Fixed Loop** button and enter "1" in the box. Enter a higher value to repeat the sequence a fixed number of times.

  Click the **Endless Loop** button to have the sequence repeat indefinitely.

- If the playback of certain frames (or all frames) seems too fast, you can select any frame and enter a value greater than 0 in the **Frame Delay** field. The frame's delay factor (in milliseconds) will be exported along with the GIF. Sometimes all frames may require a delay factor in order to achieve proper pacing. You can select multiple (or all) frames and enter a common value in the Frame Delay field.

To stop the animation:

- Click the □ **Stop** button.

To export the animation as a GIF file:

● Choose **Export Optimizer...** from the **File** menu. The animated GIF format is selected as default.

For details on exporting, see Exporting to another file format on p. 213.

To preview the animation in your web browser:

● Choose **Preview in Browser** from the **File** menu. PhotoPlus exports the image as a temporary file, then opens the file for preview in your web browser.

To flatten your frames:

● For more complex animations, your animation project can be simplified by flattening all frames (individual frames cannot be flattened); right-click and choose **Flatten Frames**. Multiple layers associated with frames are replaced by a single layer; layer objects are no longer independent and are therefore no longer editable.

10 Pressure Sensitivity &
Pen Tablets

Pressure sensitivity

Pressure sensitivity is a property of individual brushes, and is only applicable if you're a pen tablet user.

Task:	Using:
• retouch photos by painting out specific areas.	Paintbrush Tool
• retouch photos by erasing specific areas.	Standard Eraser Tool Background Eraser Tool
• retouch photos to lighten and darken areas.	Dodge Tool Burn Tool
• creatively paint over photos for stylistic effect (e.g., Matte painting).	Paintbrush Tool

In simple terms, pressure sensitivity means that your brush stroke changes in size, opacity, etc., in proportion with the amount of pressure you apply using your tablet's input device (e.g., Pressure Stylus, Eraser, or Airbrush).

For more information about tablets, see Using pen tablets (p. 198).

Enabling pressure sensitivity

Where appropriate, only selected PhotoPlus brushes are pressure sensitive by default (i.e., Basic, Calligraphic, Stamps, and selected Effects or Media brushes). Some brushes are not pressure sensitive because of their inherent characteristics (e.g., spray brushes).

For the tablet user, you normally don't need to do anything apart from paint or draw with your pressure-sensitive device. This is because the attributes of **Size** and **Opacity** for those selected brushes are already pressure-enabled.

However, for less-commonly used attributes such as **Spacing** and **Shape**, pressure is disabled by default, although you can **manually** switch on pressure sensitivity for these brush attributes at any time via the brush's Context toolbar (Brush Options), and optionally save the brush as a tool preset for future use (see PhotoPlus Help).

Using pen tablets

You can either draw or paint with your mouse or, for a more natural experience, use a **pen tablet**. A pen tablet is comprised of an intelligent electronic pad equipped with pressure-sensitive input devices (e.g., Pressure Stylus and Eraser). A rectangular "active" area responds to pressure applied by that input device.

The pad, when connected to your computer, allows sketching, freehand line drawing and painting within PhotoPlus, making the drawing experience truly realistic. The tablet's pressure-sensitive capabilities in conjunction with PhotoPlus allows control of stroke width or opacity when drawing or painting.

PhotoPlus works equally well from entry-level to professional pen tablets from all the major tablet manufacturers including Wacom® and AipTek.

Within PhotoPlus, you can use the **Pressure Studio** to calibrate your tablet's pressure response and to customize your own assignments for your tablet's ExpressKeys*, TouchStrip*, or TouchRing*. PhotoPlus settings take precedence over your device's original settings.

* Not available on some pen tablets.

Using Pressure Studio

PhotoPlus's Pressure Studio acts as an interface between your tablet and PhotoPlus, purposely designed to:

- Calibrate pressure response (below) for multiple input devices, so that PhotoPlus tools respond more predictably per device.

- Set up your tablet's key assignments from within PhotoPlus (if your tablet supports function keys).

The studio offers:

- a **practice area** for automatically calibrating your tablet's input devices (Pressure Stylus, Eraser, Airbrush, etc.) by drawing soft/firm strokes. Manual calibration for fine-tuning is also possible. As you swap between each device (e.g., between stylus and eraser) the pressure response curve for that device is displayed accordingly.

- Management of pressure **response profiles**. Preset profiles are available to resolve common problems associated with unexpected pressure response.

- **Enabling/Disabling of pressure input globally**, to allow PhotoPlus to operate with/without tablet pressure sensitivity. When enabled globally, Basic, Calligraphic, Stamps, and selected Effects or Media brushes become pressure sensitive to brush size and opacity by default.

To launch Pressure Studio:

- Select ![icon] **Pressure Studio** from the **Standard** toolbar.

> Before calibration, practise drawing with your input device in the practice area!

The calibration process is described in detail in the PhotoPlus Help.

Function key assignment

If your pen tablet is equipped with ExpressKeys (or equivalent), Pressure Studio lets you assign your tablet's keys to PhotoPlus tools. The studio changes depending on the type of pen tablet installed, so you'll get an accurate representation of your pen tablet's key layout shown within Pressure Studio's **Functions tab**.

Example of Wacom Intuos 3's ExpressKey assignment in PhotoPlus.

💡 Can't see your Functions tab? This is only displayed when your pen tablet is plugged in and operational (and possesses function keys).

To customize your function keys:

1. With the Functions tab in view, select an alternative tool from the drop-down list. Pressing the appropriate key on your tablet will activate that tool in PhotoPlus.

2. Click **OK**.

To revert to the tablet's default key assignment:

1. Select the "Tablet Default" option from a specific key's drop-down list.

2. Click **OK**.

⭐ For Wacom Intuos4® users, your tablet will intelligently display currently assigned PhotoPlus tool icons next to your ExpressKeys.

11 Printing & Exporting

Printing

For basic printing primarily to desktop printers, **Print Studio** offers an exciting, comprehensive, and versatile printing solution for your photos.

Print Mode — Print Mode Options — Page Layout — Templates

Open Images

The easy-to-use studio environment lets you select from a variety of print templates, each designed for either **single-** or **multi-image** printing. Multi-image printing in PhotoPlus lets you make the most of expensive photo-quality printing paper by "ganging" several images onto a single output sheet using a **print layout** or **contact sheet** template (shown above).

- **Single Image templates**
  Use for basic desktop printing of an individual image, with supporting Layout options (custom or standard print sizes, positioning, tiling, and image-to-cell fitting).

- **Print Layout templates**

  Use for multi-image standard print sizes (in portrait/landscape orientation), passport sizes, and mixed print sizes.

- **Contact Sheet templates**

  Use for multi-image template-driven thumbnail prints—great for creating labels!

> For any mode, you can also create your own custom template from an existing template.

> Currently open documents will be used for printing, although you can add more directly within Print Studio.

To print (using templates):

1. Click the 🖨 **Print** button on the **Standard** toolbar.

   The Print Studio appears.

2. (Optional) To open additional images for printing, click **Add Images...**. Select a photo for addition then click **Open...**. The images are added as a thumbnail to the gallery.

3. From the right-hand templates list, select a template category, e.g. Single Images (Portrait).

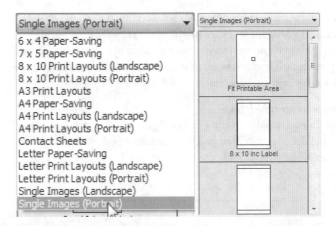

4. To insert a particular template into the central page layout region, simply click its gallery thumbnail.

5. Depending on print mode, decide on which image(s) are to be used for printing, i.e.

   - For **Single Image** templates, you can select a different image from the lower image gallery.

   - For **Print Layout** templates, right-click a gallery thumbnail and select **Fill Layout with Image**. All occupied or empty cells in your layout are replaced. Alternatively, to fill an individual cell, drag a replacement image from the lower image gallery onto the "target" cell. A print layout's cells need to be manually populated; other modes will auto-populate cells.

   - For **Contact Sheet** templates, use the **Distribution** option in **Image Options** to control image replacement.

6. (Optional) From the left-hand pane, click the ▷ button to expand **Image Options** for sizing and rotating images in cells:

   - Enable **Fit image to cell** to make the image fit within the cell boundaries.

   - Enable **Fill cell with image** to scale the image to fit all of the cell.

   - Check **Rotate for best fit** to make portrait images fit cells of landscape orientation (and vice versa) to make maximum use of cell space.

7. (Optional) Check **Border** to add a border of a configurable width (use input box) and **Colour** (click the swatch to select colour from a dialog).

8. (Optional) To caption your images, check **Label** to add a Date, image Filename, or Sequence number under each image; select from the drop-down menu. For a combination of label formats, click **Modify...**, add tokens to assemble a sample name, then click **OK**; the drop-down menu changes to Custom. See Changing file names for more information.

9. Click **Print...** or **Close** to save settings (but not print).

If you want to create your own layouts instead of templates you can switch print modes and customize settings for that mode.

To print using your own layouts:

1. Click the 🖶 **Print** button on the **Standard** toolbar.

    The Print Studio appears.

2. From the **Mode** drop-down list, select Single Image, Print Layout, or Contact Sheet.

    ▽ General

    Mode: Single Image ▼
    Single Image
    Printer: Print Layout
    Contact Sheet
    Print Setup

3. In the Layout section, select a custom or standard print **Size**.

4. (Optional) Follow image sizing and rotating instructions described above.

To store the current page layout with images:

*   Click **Save Layout...** on the image gallery. PhotoPlus saves your layout exactly as is, with or without images in the cells.

To open a new layout, click **Open Layout...** on the gallery.

To store the current page layout as a template without images:

*   Right-click on the right-hand template list to pop up a menu that lets you add or delete templates and categories. After creating a custom category using **Add Category...** (or selecting an existing category), right-click to save your template exactly as is (without images in the cells) by using **Add Template...**.

🔖 Print modes are reset each time PhotoPlus is restarted. Changes you make during a session are only "remembered" for the duration of the session.

Sizing and rotating images in cells

▽ Image Options

◉ Fit image to cell   ○ Fill cell with image

☐ Rotate for best fit

The Print dialog helps you size or rotate your image(s) to fit a cell(s) according to **Image Options** settings.

When the dialog is opened, the default settings above will be adopted. It's likely that some fine tuning might be needed, e.g. a portrait image may best be rotated to fit a cell of landscape orientation.

If further images are added from the image gallery, they will also adopt these settings. You can select an individual cell to affect the scaling or rotation on that cell only at a later time. To again apply a setting to all cells, first deselect a cell by clicking outside the grid.

Here's a visual breakdown of the different options.

Fit image to cell/Fill cell with image

These options toggle respectively between fitting the image to cell dimensions (it will scale the image width to cell width or image height to cell height) or making the image completely fill the cell, losing portions of the image from view.

Fit image to cell
enabled

Fill cell with image
enabled

Rotate for best fit

You can re-orient your image to fit cells using the **Rotate for best fit** check box—great for fitting a portrait image into landscape-oriented cells (and vice versa).

Rotate for best fit
unchecked

Rotate for best fit
checked

Cropping images in cells

If you're looking to be more specific about which areas of your image to print, you can crop your image instead of using the above Image Options. PhotoPlus supports some sophisticated cropping options, especially the ability to crop using the image or the image's cell dimensions.

To crop an image:

1. From the dialog, select an image from the lower gallery and click **Crop Image...**.

2. From the Crop Image dialog, choose an **Aspect Ratio** from the drop-down menu which dictates the proportions of your crop area grid: **Unconstrained** creates a grid which can be proportioned in any way; **Cell** matches to cell dimensions; **Image** maintains image dimensions; **Custom** uses a custom constrained ratio (e.g., a square) that you define yourself in the adjacent input boxes.

	Before	After
Unconstrained		
Cell		
Image (default)		
Custom (e.g., 1.00 x 1.00 in)		

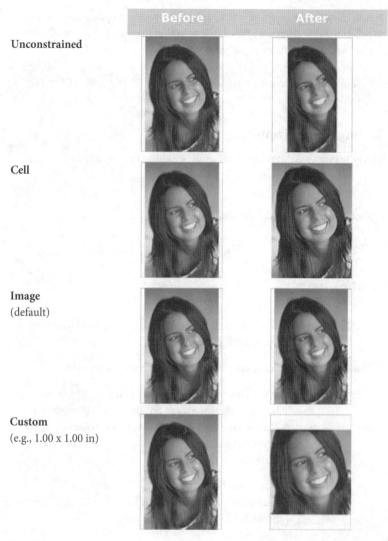

3. Drag a crop area's corner to size your crop according to requirements, then move the grid around the image to choose the preferred image area to be cropped. To revert, click **Clear** to reset your crop grid.

4. Click **OK**.

If your image is already present in your layout then it will update automatically to reflect the new cropping applied. If it hasn't yet been used, the crop is still applied to the image in the image gallery.

 Cropping affects every instance of the image. Once applied, all images are updated.

Setting viewing options

The following global viewing options will be applied to every page.

View Options	
☑ Show Cells ☐ Show Margins	
☐ Grid: 0.50 in ▲▼	Colour: ▮
Units: inches ▼	

Show Cells	When checked, each cell border is displayed within which the image is placed.
Show Margins	When checked, margin guides are shown in blue.
Grid	When checked, a dot snapping grid is applied to the layout—cells will snap to the grid to aid cell positioning. Use the input box and/or **Colour** swatch to enter a grid interval (spacing) or pick a different grid colour via a dialog.
Units	Use the drop-down menu to select a different measurement unit used in the Layout and Image Options panes.

For professional printing, the Separations and Prepress options control CMYK colour separations and printer marks.

Printing using colour separations

The Separations and Prepress options, shown for every mode, are used for professional printing with CMYK colour separations. This process is now a less popular printing method compared to electronic PDF publishing (using PDF/X1 compliance). See PhotoPlus Help for more details.

Publishing a PDF file

PhotoPlus can output your drawings to PDF (Portable Document Format), a cross-platform WYSIWYG file format developed by Adobe, intended to handle documents in a device- and platform-independent manner.

PDF documents are ideal for both screen-ready distribution and professional printing. In PhotoPlus, ready-to-go PDF profiles are available for both uses, making PDF setup less complicated.

- **Screen-ready**. If you require screen-ready PDFs you're likely to need PDF documents which use Acrobat compatibility and an RGB colour space, along with optional document security.

- **Professional**. PDF documents are also suited to professional printing, i.e. when you deliver your artwork to a print partner (normally external to your company). You'll typically require PDF/X-1a compatibility (for CMYK output)and prepress page marks.

  To make things simple, the professional print profile called "PDF X-1a" is provided in PhotoPlus (using PDF X-1a compatibility), but you should check with your print partner if PDF/X-1, and any other settings, may be required instead.

  With PDF/X-1a or PDF/X-1 compatibility, colours will be output in the CMYK colour space, and fonts you've used will be embedded. A single PDF/X file will contain all the necessary information your print partner requires.

To export a PhotoPlus picture as a PDF:

1. Choose **Publish as PDF...** from the **File** menu to display the **Publish PDF** dialog.

2. Set basic output options on the dialog's **General** tab (shown).

   - Checking **Fit to complete page** or **Fit to page width** to set the default page view when the PDF is opened in Acrobat Reader.

   - Checking **Preview PDF file** automatically opens the PDF in a compatible PDF viewer after it's been created, so you can review it immediately. (If anything looks amiss, you'll need to fix the problems in the file and regenerate the PDF.)

   - If handing off a file to a professional printer, choose either "PDF/X-1" or "PDF/X-1a" in the **Compatibility** list as advised by your print partner (otherwise just use an Acrobat $X.0$ option, where X is the version number).

   - In the Colour Management section, the **Output colour space** setting should always be "CMYK" for professional printing; otherwise "RGB" is fine. Select the **Destination** profile recommended by your print partner.

- The **Prepress Marks** section lets you include printer marks in your PDF output (check an option to switch on). Use for professional printing.

3. Set security options (if any) on the **Security** tab.

    You can add password protection to keep the contents of your document away from unintended eyes, and/or lock certain capabilities to prevent unauthorized dissemination or changes. For example, you can specify **No document printing** to prevent paper reproduction of the publication's contents, or **No content copying** to help ensure your work can't be easily duplicated somewhere else. You can even enter a master password to give you—and only you—the right to alter these security settings. (Just be sure to remember your password!)

4. Click **OK**.

Exporting to another file format

In many situations, you'll want to save a file to one of the standard graphics formats. In PhotoPlus, this is known as **exporting**.

JPEG ▼
Autotraced Metafile
Graphic Interchange Format
HD Photo
JPEG
JPEG 2000 (J2K)
JPEG 2000 (JP2)
Kodak Flash Pix
Macintosh PICT
PhotoShop
Portable Network Graphic
Sun Raster Image
Tagged Image File
Truevision TARGA
Windows Bitmap
WordPerfect Graphic
ZSoft PaintBrush

Exporting an image means converting it to a specified graphic file format other than the native PhotoPlus (.spp) format. This flattens the image, removing layer information.

Only the SPP and the Photoshop PSD formats preserves image information, such as multiple layers, masks, or image map data that would be lost in conversion to another format.

The Export process itself can be carried out by using either a standard file dialog where you can specify the path, name and format of the image file, or by using an **Export Optimizer** where you can additionally compare export previews for multiple file formats before export.

To export an image:

1. Choose **Export...** from the **File** menu.

2. The Export dialog appears, with the file's current base name shown. Change the base name if desired.

3. To open the Export Optimizer to fine-tune export settings, click **Optimizer**, then click **OK**.

4. Click **Save** in the **Export** dialog.

> The Export dialog includes additional options for use with web images (see Slicing images and Creating image maps on p. 167 and p. 171).

You can also open the Export Optimizer first and (at your discretion) proceed to the exporting step after checking your settings. You can access the Export Optimizer at any time—not just at export time—to compare image quality using different settings (your settings are retained for each format).

The Export Optimizer consists of a left-hand preview display (single, dual, or quad) and a right-hand settings region, with additional View and Zoom buttons along the bottom of the dialog. Dual and quad previews let you test and compare between different export formats in each pane—simply select a preview pane and then test various quality settings, change format-specific options or resize before going ahead with your optimized file's export—it even retains your preferred settings for each format!

Preview
Displays

Format

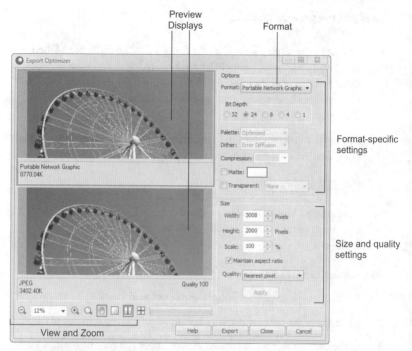

Format-specific settings

Size and quality settings

View and Zoom

To open the Export Optimizer:

1. Click **Export Optimizer...** from the **File** menu.

2. From the Export Optimizer dialog, use the **Options** section to specify the file **Format**, and format-specific options such as bit depth, dithering, palette, and compression. The **Size** section lets you scale, stretch, or squash the image, while setting an export **Quality** setting (e.g., a resampling method such as Bicubic).

3. Review your optimized image, and when you're happy with it, click **Export**. The **Close** button will instead abort the export but save any format-specific option changes made in the dialog.

4. From the Export dialog, enter a file name, and choose a file format from the drop-down list. The export format and custom settings will be remembered for future exports. Click **OK**.

To adjust the preview display:

- To change the display scale, click the dialog's 🔍 **Zoom Tool** and then left-click (to zoom in), right-click (to zoom out) on the preview, or choose a zoom percentage in the lower left in the drop-down list. You can also select a specific area by dragging a marquee around an item of interest.

- To display a different portion of the image, first select the dialog's 🖐 **Pan Tool**, then drag the image in the active preview pane.

- ▫️◻️▦ Click one of the View buttons shown below the preview pane to select **Single**, **Double**, or **Quad** display. The multi-pane (Double and Quad) settings allow for before-and-after comparison of export settings.

To compare export settings:

1. Set the preview display for either **Double** or **Quad** view.

2. Click one of the preview display panes to select it as the active pane.

3. In the Options section, choose an export format and specific settings. Each time you make a new choice, the active pane updates to show the effect of filtering using the new settings, as well as the estimated file size.

4. To compare settings, select a different display pane and repeat the process. The Export Optimizer lets you experiment freely and evaluate the results.

To revert back to a single pane, click ▫️ **Single**.

To proceed with exporting:

1.   Make sure the active preview pane is using the settings you want to apply to the image.

2.   Click the dialog's **Export** or **OK** button to display the Export dialog.

> The Export Optimizer saves settings for particular formats according to the most recent update in the Options section. In other words, if you have two or more preview panes displaying the same file format, the settings for the last of them you click in will be those associated with exporting in that format.

To preview an image in your web browser:

*   Choose **Preview in Browser...** from the **File** menu. PhotoPlus exports the image as a temporary file, then opens the file for preview in your web browser.

Sharing documents by email

PhotoPlus lets you send your currently selected document (or JPG) to your standard email program (e.g., Outlook) for subsequent mailing. You can do this by choosing **Send...** from the **File** menu to display a dialog which sets the file type and image size restrictions.

After this, a new email message is displayed with document attached. To complete the process, press the **Send** button (or equivalent) on your email program as for any other email message.

Setting the file type

To take advantage of better file compression you may want to convert your image to JPEG if not already in this format. The conversion would be suitable if your original document was in TIF format or was a very complex multi-layered SPP file.

From the above dialog, send the original SPP file by enabling the **Keep Original** radio button. To convert to JPEG and send as such, enable **Convert to JPEG**.

Setting your image size

By default, PhotoPlus sends any photo with a file size limiter applied. This avoids sending excessively large files! You can optionally select an alternative image resolution—this will be the new pixel height or width (the biggest pixel dimension of the original photo will be reduced to the new image size)

Uncheck the **Limit image dimensions to a maximum of** check box to keep original image dimensions.

An Internet connection is required to email pictures.

12 PhotoPlus Organizer:
Getting Started

Organizing photos

PhotoPlus Organizer is Serif's powerful photo management application which acts as an essential launch point for your photos. From your collection of photos you'll be able to perform a range of **management** and **filtering** operations.

To launch Organizer:

1. Display PhotoPlus's Startup Wizard.

2. Select **Open PhotoPlus Organizer**. Organizer is launched as a separate application.

    OR

-   From the **Standard** toolbar, select 🔘 **Organizer**.

> Press your **F1** key to view PhotoPlus Organizer Help.

Adding photos

Adding photos to Organizer simply means opening a "window" to your operating system. All you have to do is to include the photos' folders in Organizer—you'll then see the photos displayed in your workspace. Your photos **always** remain in their original location and unchanged while using Organizer.

Organizer lets you:

- **Add** photos directly from your computer disk.

  and:

- **Import** (then **add**) photos from a USB device (cameras, flash drives) or DVD.

The procedures for both methods differ slightly. For the former, the photo addition is straightforward—files are always available. For the latter, you have to import photos to your hard drive first.

Adding photos from disk

To add photos from a hard disk:

1. From the Organize tab, under the **All photos** section, click **Include folder**.

2. In the **Browse for Folder** dialog, navigate to, then select the folder containing your photos.

3. Click **OK**.

The photos from the chosen folder will be added to the Photos pane, with the folder name being added to the Organize tab.

> Users typically organize photos in specific folders. By including these folders rather than individual files you have a quick and easy process for building up your photos for organizing.

> Organizer is automatically set up to "watch" any folder you have included. This means that any photos added subsequently to the included folder are displayed in Organizer as they are added.

Importing files from USB device or DVD

Photos may be imported into Organizer from a camera, scanner or removable USB flash drive at any time. The process involves the transfer of photos from the device to a user–defined file folder. The photos are then automatically added to your Organizer workspace.

Photos on DVD (or CD) are imported, then added, in the same manner.

To import photos from your camera, scanner or removable USB drive:

1. From the **Standard** toolbar, select  **Import**.

2. From the dialog, select a source for your files (if more than one source exists) in the **From** drop-down list.

Device

From: | Canon EOS 450D ▼ | Found - 678 photos

The Photos window will be populated with photos on the selected device.

To exclude photos from import, uncheck the check box on the photo's thumbnail.

3. Specify a target **Folder** location to which your photos will be transferred from your device. By default, this will be your My Pictures folder. Alternatively, use the [...] **Browse...** button to select a different folder; your last used folder will always be used.

4. (Optional) Select a **Subfolder** option to import photos to a named **Custom** subfolder (enter a name in the input box) or to a subfolder based on the date and/or time (of photo or current day).

5. (Optional) Uncheck **Add Folders to Organizer** if you don't want the folders (and their photos) to automatically appear in Organizer on import.

6. (Optional) For file naming, keep the **Filename** set to Keep Device Name, to ensure filenames are as they appear on your device, e.g. IMG4357.JPG. Instead, you can customize file naming using the drop-down list. You can base naming on a custom name with an n+1 interation, dates and times, or a subfolder name.

7. (Optional) Check **After Transfer Delete Originals** if you want the source photos removed automatically from the device after transfer. The **After Transfer Stack in Organizer** option, when checked, will stack your imported photos' thumbnails on top of each other, according to the photo's date taken time or time duration (click **Settings**).

8. Under **Descriptive tags** you can create and attach tags to selected photos prior to import. See Tagging photos on import.

9. Click **OK**.

During import, a progress bar is displayed. If needed, click ✖ **Cancel** to stop the import process. Photos are imported to the chosen folder, and appear in Organizer.

To import photos from a DVD (or CD):

1. As above, but select **Browse...** in the **From** drop-down list.

2. From the dialog, navigate to, then select the DVD or CD containing your photos.

3. Click **OK**.

4. Follow the procedure from Step 4 on p. 224.

Creating smart albums

Organizer is designed for simplicity and ease of use. For the most part, you can tag, rate, and manipulate photos in your Photos pane—photos display if you've included them from chosen folders (see p. 222).

A further feature of Organizer is the ability to create **smart albums**. These are collections of photos that are created and stored as a result of a search for photos that possess inherent photo properties. Searches could include only specific Date Taken times, File Format, Width, Height, Name, and Path. Smart album creation also lets you build up multiple search conditions that can subject to an "AND" or "OR" operation.

To create a smart album:

1. From the Organize tab, click **Create album**.

2. From the dialog, enter an **Album Name**.

Album Name

Namibia Wildlife

3. Enable a **Search Condition**. this will apply an "AND" or "OR" condition on multiple search conditions.

4. From the drop-down list, select a photo property.

Date Taken
Date Taken
Place Taken
File Format
Width
Height
File Size
Orientation
Rating
Tagged With
Name
Path

The adjacent drop-down lists change according to the type of search condition chosen. For example, the Date Taken condition can be set to be on, before, after, between, or since a set date.

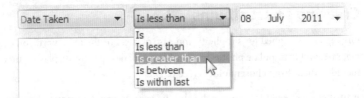

5. Click **Add**. The search condition is added to the list box.

6. Repeat from Step 4. Each further search condition is added to the search condition list.

7. Click **OK** to exit the dialog. The album is created and added to the Smart albums section of the Organize tab.

To edit a smart album:

1. Right-click the album name in the Organize tab and select **Edit Album...**.

2. For renaming, edit the Album Name.

3. To change any search condition, double-click it, edit the upper drop-down lists, and click **Update**.

To delete a smart album:

- Right-click the album name in the Organize tab and select **Delete Album....**
  You'll be prompted to confirm that you want to delete the album.

Editing photos in Serif PhotoPlus

If you own Serif PhotoPlus (version 10 or later) you'll be able to perform
professional editing of your photo in PhotoPlus, launched directly from within
Organizer.

To launch a photo in Serif PhotoPlus:

1. Select a photo thumbnail.

2. From the Organizer's **Standard** toolbar, select **Edit in PhotoPlus**.
   Serif PhotoPlus will be launched automatically (if installed).

3. Make your image adjustment in PhotoPlus, ensuring that you use the **Save**
   or **Save Original** (depending on your version of PhotoPlus) option on the
   PhotoPlus File menu to save your file. Changes made will be shown in
   Organizer—your photo thumbnail will update automatically.

13 PhotoPlus Organizer:
Managing Photos

Managing folders

Your folder structure in Windows may be just how you want it. However, Organizer makes an easy job of creating and managing folders directly from the Organize tab.

You'll then be able to drag and drop photos into your new folders, creating a new Windows folder hierarchy from within Organizer.

To create a new folder:

1. From the Organize tab, right-click an existing folder name and select **New Folder** from the flyout.

2. Enter a folder name in the highlighted text, overwriting the "New folder" text.

3. Press the Return key.

A folder can be created from any folder in Organizer, always being created as a subfolder.

Once created, you'll be able to manage your folders in various ways, from the same flyout.

- **Open Folder**: Opens a standard Windows folder.

- **Rename Folder**: Changes the Windows folder name.

- **Delete Folder**: Deletes the current folder.

Viewing photos

There are many ways in which you can view your photos:

- In the **Photos** pane, double-click a thumbnail to see it at the maximum size that will fit to the Photo pane (or pressing **Ctrl-Tab** on a selected thumbnail). Double-click again to minimize.

- Use the **Page Up** or **Page Down** keys on your keyboard.

- Your mouse may have a wheel which will allow you to scroll up/down your thumbnail window or jump to the next or previous photo.

- Use the Zoom tools on the Status Bar, to zoom to photos in increments or via slider.

- The photo can be launched in Serif PhotoPlus (see Editing your photos in PhotoPlus on p. 227)—especially if you want to perform some advanced editing of the photo. Also open your photo in Serif PanoramaPlus or Serif CraftArtist.

Selecting thumbnails

Before looking at each of the operations that can be used to manage your photos it's worthwhile familiarizing yourself with the different options available for selecting thumbnails. Selection is the pre-cursor to performing an operation.

The main methods of selection are:

- **Single click:** A click on the thumbnail will make it selected so that the thumbnail is shaded in grey.

- **Drag select:** This can typically be used for selecting more than one thumbnail simultaneously. Click next to a thumbnail, hold your mouse button down and drag over your required thumbnails. Release the mouse button when you're happy with the selection.

- To select all displayed photos, use **Ctrl**+A.

- If your photos are grouped, double-click the group's title bar to select all photo thumbnails in that group.

Resizing thumbnails

Several methods can be used to set thumbnail sizes to your preferred dimensions.

- Double-click the thumbnail to "maximize" it to the **Photos** pane. If you double-click again, it will revert back to its original size.

-

  Use the magnification slider on the Status Bar to zoom in or out. Alternatively, click on the adjacent **Zoom Out** and **Zoom In** icons for magnification in increments. The aspect ratio for each thumbnail is maintained.

- Use "+" and "-" on your keyboard to increase or decrease the size of selected thumbnails in small increments.

Changing thumbnail display

By default, your photos will display in Organizer as simple thumbnails. However, you can add useful additional photo information, called **content fields**, to each thumbnail such as Time Taken, Date Taken, Current Rating, and a Geotag indicator.

thumbnail	*thumbnail*
(no information)	*(information)*

To display photo information on thumbnails:

1. Select your photo thumbnail(s).

2. From the **View** menu, select **Content Fields**, and choose the content field to be displayed from the flyout.

> Name
> Time Taken
> Date Taken
> Rating
> Geo-Tag

In this example, only the Rating field will be displayed.

💡 If you click the 📍 **Show on Google Map** icon, the location that your photo was taken is shown in MapMode View.

Changing photo order

The thumbnails displayed in Organizer can be sorted using the following sort criteria:

- **Date Taken** (time that photo was taken; from Exif)

- **File Creation Time** (time copied to hard disk)

- **File Modified Time**

- **Rating**

> The file date and times for the selected photo are displayed in the Metadata tab.

Photos can be ordered in ascending order which shows the oldest photos first and descending order which shows the newest.

To change photo order:

1. From the **View** menu, select a sort option from the **Sort By** menu flyout.

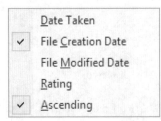

2. Select a different sort type, e.g. File Creation Time.

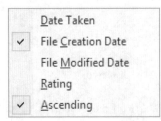

3. (Optional) To reverse the order (i.e., Descending), uncheck **Ascending**.

Grouping photos

The thumbnails displayed in Organizer can be grouped using the following grouping criteria.

- **Auto**: Groups according to what is selected in the Organize tab (default).

- **Folder**. The folder name within which photos are located.

- **Date Taken**. The date and time that photos were taken (from Exif).

- **File Type**. The file type of photos, e.g. JPEG or PNG.

- **Rating**. The rating previously assigned to photos.

- **Tag**. The tags previously assigned to photos.

- **None**. Photos are not grouped.

To group photos:

1. From the **View** menu, select **Group By** to reveal a menu flyout.

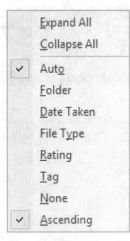

This example would group thumbnails by whatever is selected in the Organize tab. For example, you'll get a grouping of just 5 star photos, if you only click the 5 star option. For more than one selected tag, date, and rating, the grouping will be according to the first clicked option.

2. Select a different grouping, e.g. Rating.

3. (Optional) To reverse the order (i.e., Descending), uncheck **Ascending**.

Stacking photos

Organizer allows you to stack photo thumbnails on top of each other to further organize thumbnails on display. You may want to gather photos together for several reasons:

- To group by similar subject matter, e.g. all your photos of a leopard.

- For workflow, where deficient stacked photos can be tagged as "To Fix".

- For stacking a generated panorama and its source photos.

- For stacking "bracketed" photos taken at different exposures.

To create stacked photos:

- From the **Standard** toolbar, click ⬚ **Stack**.

The photo stack is clearly indicated by a white border. An Expand button (indicated), when clicked, reveals all the photos in the stack. Click the Collapse button to stack again.

When you import photos from USB devices, Organizer allows you to automatically create stacks of photos based on dates/times or duration.

To unstack a selected photo stack:

- From the **Standard** toolbar, click ⬚ **Unstack**.

To set which photo shows at top of stack:

- From an expanded stack, right-click the photo and select **Set Stack Top** from the **Stack** flyout. When the stack is collapsed, your chosen photo displays.

To add more photos to your stack:

- Drag and drop a photo onto your stack.

Rotating and flipping photos

For more advanced digital cameras, a photo's orientation (portrait/landscape) is detected and stored automatically in the photo's Exif data. This means that Organizer will be able to auto-rotate such photos to their correct orientation as soon as they are imported into your album.

However, for legacy digital content, photo acquisition from more basic cameras, and scanned images, you'll have to manually rotate your photo to its intended orientation; typically by a rotation of 90° clockwise. Of course, you may choose to rotate any photo for artistic reasons at any time.

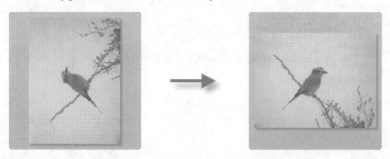

To rotate a selected photo in 90° intervals:

- From the **Standard** toolbar, click **Rotate Left** or **Rotate Right**.

To flip a selected photo horizontally or vertically:

- Select **Horizontal Flip** or **Vertical Flip** from the **Edit** menu's **Flip** flyout.

Creating tags

Tags may be added to the Organize tab automatically when adding photos tagged previously (see p. 241). However, for more personalized tagging it's possible to manually **create your own** tags from the same tab.

You can also use **preset** "action-based" tags to help identify photos which require further action, e.g. Reviewed, To Print, To Fix, and To Share. Like custom tags you can assign these to your photos by drag and drop.

With any of the above tagging methods, you'll then be able to use one of the most powerful features of Organizer—Filter by tag (see p. 260).

To create tags:

1. From the Organize tab, click the down arrow on the Descriptive tags entry.

2. Select **Create Tag**.

3. Type a new tag name in the highlighted text box.

   The tag structure is update to display your new tag.

To create a tag hierarchy:

You can nest tags within tags for "parent-child" tagging—simply drag one tag onto another. A typical example would be placing holiday years under a general Holidays tag.

> 💡 There is no limit to the depth of tagging allowed.

> 💡 Tags can be promoted to a higher level by dragging to a "grandparent" tag or onto the top-level "Descriptive tags" label.

To rename a tag:

1. Right-click a tag name and select **Rename Tag**.

2. Type a new tag name in the highlighted text box.

To assign a tag to a thumbnail:

1. In the Photos pane, select the thumbnail(s) which are to be assigned your new tag. Blue shading will appear around the selected thumbnail(s).

2. Drag your selection onto a tag name in the Organize tab.

Alternatively, you can drag a tag name over any already selected photos.

OR

Right-click on one or more selected thumbnails, select **Attach Tag**, then select a tag name from the submenu.

Your assigned photos can then be displayed by tag name. See Filter by tag on p. 260.

To remove tags from thumbnails:

- Right-click on one or more selected thumbnails, select **Detach Tag**, then select the tag to be removed.

Rating photos

Any photo can be allocated its own star rating. This is really useful when you want to categorize your favourites—you simply assign a rating to your photos and subsequently filter your photos by rating. See Filter by rating (see p. 262).

Ratings can be from one star to five stars (maximum); five stars would normally be allocated to your most favourite photos.

To rate your photos in the Photo pane:

1. Select one or more thumbnails.

2. Drag your selection onto a rating level in the Organize tab.

Alternatively, you can drag a rating level over any selected photos.

OR

Right-click any selected thumbnail and assign a star rating from the **Set Rating** menu flyout.

To unassign a star rating:

● Right-click the selected thumbnail(s) and choose **Not Rated** from the **Set Rating** menu flyout.

Changing date and time

Most photos have date and time settings associated with them, obtained from your camera's EXIF data. The most important setting is the date and time that photo was taken, which is displayed as the **Date Taken** setting in Organizer's Metadata tab.

The Date Taken setting can be modified for several reasons.

● When on holiday or business, your digital camera's time zone settings were not adjusted—meaning that the Date Taken setting is incorrect.

● If you have a photo that was scanned, although the file creation date will be used, you can update the setting to reflect the time the photo was taken rather than when it was scanned.

For information on how to filter by date, see Filter By date (on p. 258).

To change a photo's Date Taken setting:

1. Display the Metadata tab.

2. Double-click the **Date Taken** field.

File Name: Jan_Joubert's_Gat_Bridg...
Date Taken: 17/08/2008 13:26:24
Dimensions: 1280 × 857

3. Select a date or time that you want to set for the photo.

The time is always displayed as the 24-hr clock.

Changing time zones

Suppose you're on holiday and in your excitement you forget to adjust the time settings on your digital camera upon arrival—assuming you've gone somewhere hot, sunny and far away! You've returned home to find that photo's Date Taken settings are incorrect. Don't panic—it is possible to adjust this date/time.

To change a photo's time zone:

1. In the **Photos** pane, click to select photo thumbnail(s).

2. From the **Edit** menu, select **Time Zone...**.

3. From the **Time Zone** dialog, select **Date Taken** from the **Type** drop-down list.

4. Change the date and time:

   • **relative** to the currently set **Date taken** (see below).

     OR

   • by selecting a **specific date** and time (all selected photos will be set to exactly the same time and date).

For example, the above dialog will fix photos with an incorrect date and time when taken on a holiday in Australia (+11 hours ahead of Greenwich Mean Time).

Setting a specific date and time may be preferred if calculating the difference between the photo's currently set Date Taken time and the required date is too complicated, or if you know the exact date/time for your photos, e.g. those from a New Year celebration.

 If the **Specific** date/time adjustment is used, all selected photos will have exactly the same time and date as both date and time will be applied.

 The **Relative** date/time adjustment is better when adjusting multiple images in one batch as it preserves the time differences between each image.

Instead of the default Date Taken time, you can also update times for different time types (i.e., File Creation Time or File Modified Time) via the **Type** drop-down list.

Deleting photos

Photos can be deleted at any time—you'll actually be deleting the photo from your computer, so caution should be taken.

To delete a photo:

1. Select your photo thumbnail(s).

2. From the **Edit** menu, select **Delete**.

⚠ This method will permanently delete the original file from your computer.

You'll get a confirmation message asking if you want to delete your photos from disk. If **Yes** is selected, your photo(s) will be sent to your recycle bin (restore from there if you want to revert).

Viewing and adding metadata

Organizer displays essential photo and file information exclusively in the Metadata tab. This information is a mix of EXIF and IPTC metadata.

This information comprises:

- **File properties** (File Name, Dimensions)

- **Photo properties*** (Date Taken)

- **Photo information** (Caption, Tags, Rating, Author, Copyright)

- **Camera specifications*** (make and model)

- **Shoot details*** (ISO rating, Focal Length, Exposure, Aperture, Shutter Speed, Flash, White Balance, etc.).

* When using your digital camera, this EXIF information is associated with your photo irrespective of its file format (RAW, JPG, or otherwise).

To display metadata for a selected photo:

- Display the Metadata tab.

The metadata is arranged into name/value fields, of which some are editable, e.g. Date Taken, Tags, Rating, Author, Copyright, and Caption.

To modify metadata:

- Double-click on one of the fields and type or paste new text.

Advanced View

You can display a detailed breakdown of your metadata in its EXIF or IPTC structure.

To display EXIF or IPTC data for a selected photo:

- From the Metadata tab, select the drop-down arrow next to either **More Exif** or **More Iptc**.

The tab expands to reveal EXIF and IPTC metadata in separate sections.

Geo-Tagging in MapMode View

MapMode View displays a Google™ map pane in the main area of your workspace. This allows you to navigate your Google map, view Geo-tagged photos automatically placed on your map (as pins), and then view photos in turn. Organizer also lets you manually position non-geo-tagged photos on your map easily.

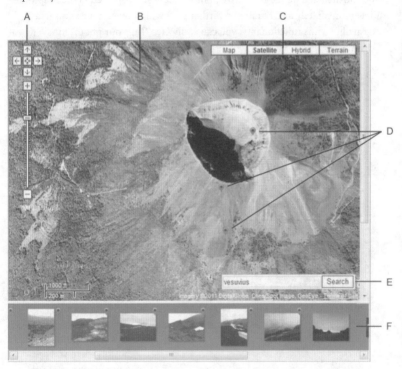

(A) Zoom/Pan tool, (B) Map pane, (C) Map Type toolbar, (D) Geo-Tag pins, (E) Map Search box, (F) Photos pane.

To display MapMode View:

* From the **Standard** toolbar, click 📍 **Map Mode**.

💡 To jump back to ThumbMode view, click ⬚⬚⬚ **Thumb Mode** on the **Standard** toolbar.

Geo Tagging

Geo-Tagging is the process of adding geographical location data to your photos. The Geo-Tag data is contained within the photo's Exif metadata.

There are a few cameras on the market that can automatically add Geo-Tag data to photos as they are taken—the Latitude and Longitude co-ordinates are written into the metadata of the respective photos. These are displayed in the MapMode View immediately and require no further editing. However, if your camera doesn't have this functionality, you can easily Geo-Tag your photos in Organizer.

To add Geo-Tag data by drag and drop:

1. Find the photo location on the map.

2. Zoom into the appropriate level on the map.

3. Select your photo(s) from the **Photos** pane and drag onto the map. Use **Ctrl**-click or **Shift**-click to select non-adjacent or adjacent photos, respectively.

4. Release the mouse button when you are happy with the position.

Geo-Tagged photos are represented in MapMode View by red pins, displayed on the map. Multiple photos will show as a grouping of pins.

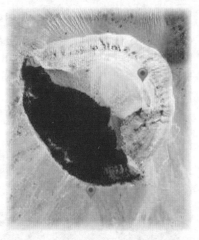

When a Geo-Tag is represented by a single pin, you can easily reposition it by dragging it to a new location. This is not possible when a group of pins is displayed.

To reposition a tag into the current map view, right-click on the selected photo thumbnail(s) and click **Add/Move Geo-Tag**. Great for moving incorrectly placed geo-tags!

Viewing information and photos

Geo-Tagged photos are represented in the **Map** pane by a red pin. Depending on the number of items associated to the Geo-Tag, and on the zoom level, these may appear as either a single pin or as a group of three pins (see below).

To view information associated with a pin:

1. Mouse over a pin, the pointer changes to a hand.

2. Click the pin to see an information bubble.

The information and options provided in the information bubble are slightly different for single photos and multiple photos. Latitude and Longitude co-ordinates are always displayed, as is the option to Delete Geo-Tag. Other displayed information may include a photo thumbnail, the number of photos associated with the Geo-Tag location, and the option to view or edit.

To view photos:

1. Click **View Photo**.

2. Photos are displayed in Full Screen View.

> You can locate geo-tagged photos by clicking the thumbnail's 💡 icon in the lower Photos pane.

> The **Show Geo-Tag** right-click option lets you view the Geo-Tag in the centre of the current map view.

To delete a Geo-Tag:

1. In ThumbMode View, select the photo thumbnail(s) with the Geo-Tag you want to remove, and right-click.

2. Select **Delete Geo-Tag**.

Smart album map boundaries

If you create smart albums (see p. 225), you can restrict your album content to photos from specific geographic areas, called **map boundaries**. These boundaries can be drawn around islands, cities, and countries, even around theme parks and venues. In fact, any geographic region where a concentration of photos have been taken.

Before creating your smart album, map boundaries need to be created.

To create map boundaries:

1. From the **Edit** menu, select **Smart Album Map Boundaries**.

2. From the dialog, zoom into the appropriate level on the map.

3.   Click repeatedly around your chosen boundary, creating white nodes as you click. Click back on the initial white node to close the area.

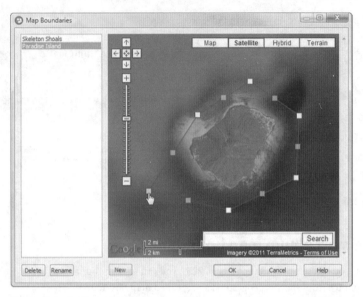

4.   In the dialog's **Name** field, add a name for your boundary, e.g. Paradise Island. A red-tinted region is created.

5.   Click **OK**.

6.   (Optional) Repeat the process for additional boundaries by clicking **New**.

> You can create map boundaries in both ThumbMode and MapMode modes.

Once you've created map boundaries, you can create a smart album which is restricted to photos taken within those chosen map boundaries. See Creating smart albums on p. 225.

14 PhotoPlus Organizer: Filtering Photos

Filtering photos

You can filter photos within Organizer by a variety of methods:

- **Folder**: Photos are filtered by the folder they are located in.

- **Date**: Photos are filtered by the date/time that the photos were originally taken.

- **Tag**: Photos are filtered by tag(s) previously assigned to your photos.

- **Rating**: Photos are filtered by a rating previously assigned.

These filtering methods are implicit when using the Organize tab—you can select one or a combination of folders, dates, tags, and ratings to create more exact filtering criteria. Use **Ctrl**-click or **Shift**-click to select multiple non-adjacent and adjacent filter entries, respectively.

You can also create your own smart albums based on a wide selection of additional photo properties, in addition to the above. See Creating smart albums. Filtering by folder, date, etc. will be applied to any selected smart album.

Filter by folder

Filter by folder lets you filter by the folders that you previously selected to be included in Organizer.

To filter photos by folder:

*   From the Organize tab, select a folder name.

    ◢ 📑 All photos
       ✚ Include folder
       📁 dump
       📁 Kew Lilies
       📁 | Namibia wildlife |
       📁 USA Holiday

The photos from that selected folder are displayed in the Photos pane.

- Use the **Shift**-click or **Ctrl**-click to include more than one adjacent or non-adjacent folder in filtering, respectively.

Filter by date

Filter by date lets you filter photos according to when photos were taken.

Your Date Taken times are present in the Organizer tab, and are initially collapsed by default. They can be revealed easily by clicking the ▷ **Expand** button.

To filter photos by date:

- From the Organize tab, select a date. This is the time that the photo was taken (see Viewing and adding metadata on p. 246).

The photos taken on that date are displayed in the Photos pane. Use the **Shift**-click or **Ctrl**-click to include more than one adjacent or non-adjacent dates in filtering, respectively.

Filter by tag

If you have assigned tags to your photos, you can use the tag to display only photos with that tag name. In Organizer, this is called **filtering**.

In advance of filtering, you can either utilize the tags within added photos, use Organizer's preset tags, or create your own user-defined tags (see p. 240). Preset tags are typically action-based to aid workflow, i.e. Reviewed, To Fix, To Print, and To Share.

Tags are present in the Organizer tab, and are initially collapsed by default. They can be revealed easily by clicking the **Expand** button.

> Descriptive tags

> ◢ Descriptive tags
>   Create tag
>   ? Not tagged
>   leopard
>   lion
>   Nature
>   Reviewed
>   To Fix
>   To Print
>   To Share

To filter by tag:

- From the **Organize tab**, select the tag name.

Photos having that tag will be displayed in the adjacent Photos pane.

In a similar manner, you can also perform multi-tag filtering, e.g., all photos tagged with "leopard" or "lion".

To filter by multiple tags:

- In the **Organize tab**, **Shift** click or **Ctrl**-click to select adjacent or non-adjacent tag names.

Not tagged status

The **Not tagged** tag will let you view photos that have no tags assigned. This can be used to separate your "processed" photos from "unprocessed" photos—newly imported photos will often not have assigned tags. As you process your photos you can keep checking the unassigned status to check your progress.

Filter by rating

Filter by rating lets you display photos that are assigned a specific "star" rating level. You can equally filter by unrated photos for future rating.

> Stars have to be assigned to photos in advance, as described in Rating your photos on p. 242.

To filter photos by rating:

- From the Organize tab, select a rating.

By default, only photos that match the rating level exactly are displayed. Use the **Shift**-click or **Ctrl**-click to include more than one adjacent or non-adjacent rating levels in filtering, respectively.

15 Index

PhotoPlus Organizer Index

Notes

Notes

Notes

Notes

Notes

Notes